All photographs are courtesy of the author or are public domain.

Nobody Ever Dies When I'm Around.

Copyright © 2016 by Jane Baker All rights reserved.

SJG & SBG & MBG &B's

<u>Sharon</u> ~ they say that behind every woman is a much smarter, stronger, calmer and taller woman. This saying has proven true in my case. Twenty years ago I met my partner in life Sharon Jo Gentry. To say that we've been through hell together is only half of it. We've been through hell together. She's been through a lot more hell dealing with me. I appreciate the tenacity and stubbornness that one must have to stay with someone so regularly annoying and peculiar. She's the best other parent someone could parent with and she's the Thelma to my Louise. Might be Louise to my Thelma. I'm not entirely sure. I do know that in that scenario I would not be driving, Sharon yells at me when I drive. It's awful really. Also I wouldn't want to be in the passenger seat because she yells when you are navigating. Come to think of it, I shouldn't get in the car. But still, a great partnership!

<u>Sam and Max</u> ~ I love you. Now stop asking if I do. It's in print.

<u>The Bakers, Cousins etc.</u> ~ I love you all, even if I don't say it. And I most likely won't.

Hello there!

In high school, I was in the play Our Town, by Thornton Wilder. I played Mrs. Webb, yet the line from that play that has always hounded me is one Emily Webb speaks after she dies and goes back to live one day again in life: "Do any human beings ever realize life while they live it—every, every minute?"

Well, of course not. No one could. The super neurotic, like myself, is cursed with a mind that tries so hard to memorize everything. From such an early age I knew this was a limited ride, and I think because of that, I remember things. This can be painful or blissful. It's usually both.

In 2002, my mother passed away. I realized then how little I knew about her life before we seven children came along. I was focused on remembering the highs and lows of my life, but my mother shared very little. Not wanting to leave my children lacking a backstory on their mom, I decided to write about my childhood as a record for them. As often happens, life got busy, and my writing fell to the side for a bit. In 2006 my eldest son, Sam was diagnosed with stage 3b Hodgkin's lymphoma. I had read that one of my favorite authors, Roald Dahl, wrote James and the Giant Peach while he attended to his son after a terrible car accident. It was then that I returned to writing about my youth, more, this time, to keep my sanity through Sam's treatment and to keep Sam laughing. No one who has heard about my childhood has had an easy time believing me. I think the saying is "True dysfunction is stranger than fictitious dysfunction." Something like that.

Spoiler Alert: my son is fine, healthy, and happy, and what came from my writing is what you have before you. I always felt that at the heart our family was very much like the Waltons, if the Walton's had a lot of dysfunction and humor was their only coping mechanism. I think you will feel the same!

It's in the memories and the writing about them that I see how many different roles I have played in my life. Sometimes I've been the hero, sometimes the asswipe, usually somewhere in between. These roles have been in tragedies, comedies, farces, and mysteries, and the roles were varied. Daughter, Sister, Cousin, Aunt, Friend, Girlfriend, Mom, Director, Teacher, Cancer Mom, Employee. If my life were my acting resume, I'd be pretty accomplished.

The result of all my memorizing and analyzing and dwelling is what I've written here. These are my memories and my thoughts, as disturbing as they may be. Enjoy.

Best Regards,

Jane

Table of Contents

Part One
Family
Chapter 1......Braces
Chapter 2......Wicker Induced Valor
Chapter 3......Cousin Carla
Chapter 4......David
Chapter 5.......Gun Safety
Chapter 6.......Learning to Drive with Bake
Chapter 7.......The Poconos
Chapter 8.......My Sister Joanne
Chapter 9.......Can forgive, hard to forget
Chapter 10.....Delores

Part Two
Friends/Skoolin
Chapter 11.....Summer Stage
Chapter 12.....Nuns
Chapter 13.....Monica My Monica
Chapter 14.....A Bit of 1985
Chapter 15.....Dracula, Starring Tina Fey

Part Three
Gay Nesssss
Chapter 16.....Gay Trade
Chapter 17.....No Longer Not Gay
Chapter 18.....Let's Go On An Outing
Chapter 19.....Sorry About Your Rainbow
Chapter 20.....Summer of Love

Part Four
Hired Hand
Chapter 21.....Procurer of Broadway Show Tickets
Chapter 22.....Governess
Chapter 23.....Telecommunications Professional
Chapter 24.....Broadway House Hotel
Chapter 25.....Stray Cat Strut at the Answering Service

Part Five
Adulthood & Mommy Time
Chapter 26.....If I Should Die
Chapter 27.....Hazed and Confused
Chapter 28.....Goodbye Joey
Chapter 29..... A Pearl of Wisdom From My Daddy-O
Chapter 30..... It Happened One Day
Chapter 31..... Daddy Day at Dartmouth
Chapter 32.....You're a Mother

Part One

Family

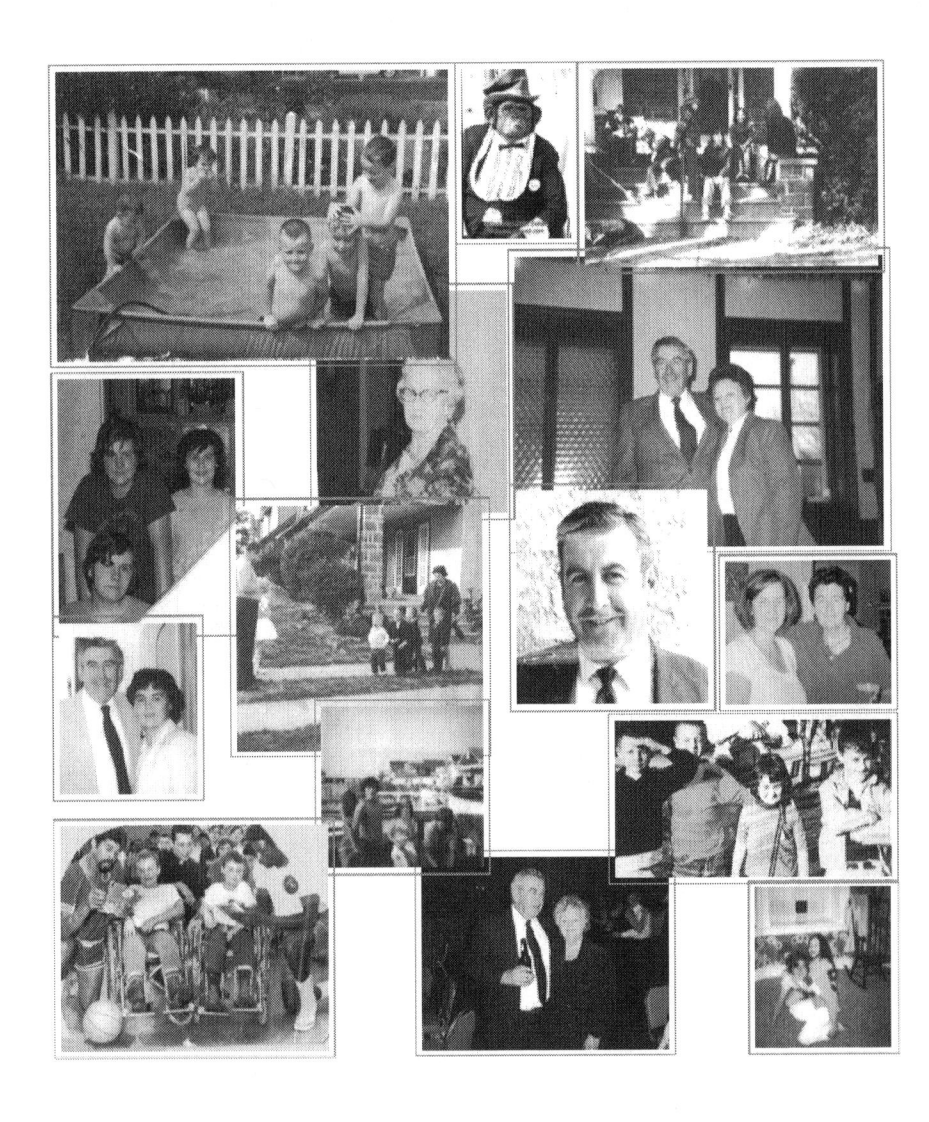

CHAPTER 1

Braces

I was six years old when my mother grabbed my younger brother Biggs and me and pulled us into a large walk-in closet. She told us that Pat and David were getting surgeries to help them walk and that after the casts came off their legs, they would have to wear braces. Then she showed us these large bulky metallic braces. Not the kind for teeth, the kind for legs. "When Pat and David come home from the hospital, they will need to wear these to walk." The brown oxford boots attached to the bottom of the hunks of metal made sense to me now. "It's very important that we don't laugh or make fun of them when they wear these, okay? They are called leg braces, so if Daddy asks you to get them for him, you will know what he means, okay?"

I was very upset and insulted by her statement. I loved my brothers; why would I make fun of them? If there was any more conversation after that, I don't remember it. I do remember standing there looking at the braces. They looked so heavy. I decided then that when I could, I would practice carrying them so I would be ready if my dad asked me to get them. Later, I snuck back in and lifted one; I could hardly pick it up. I remember thinking it was okay if they were too heavy, I wouldn't need to lift them. I don't know why I felt that way, but I was right. Neither of my brothers ever walked again after that hospital stay. I learned that the name for my brothers' illness was Duchenne muscular dystrophy. In that year, first grade, our teacher told us that if we ever needed to know anything, we could ask the librarian. I went to the librarian and asked her to tell me what muscular dystrophy was. She found a medical book and read to me what it was in great detail. I knew then that what Pat and David had was a very bad disease. I went home that day, went to my room, and cried and cried. My mother came in and asked me why I was crying, and I told her what I'd found out. "Never, never say that in this house. Never tell anyone that. Never cry about that again. They are not that sick. They will be fine. Never say that again." I never did talk about the disease in the house again. Those braces she showed us were useless, and the conversation with my mother changed my life.

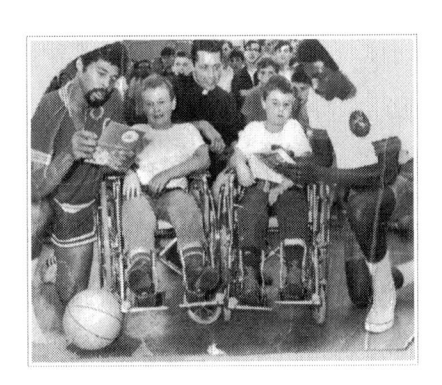

CHAPTER 2

Wicker Induced Valor

When I was probably around eleven years old (I fear it might have been closer to fourteen) I stayed overnight at my cousins' house after one of our shared Christmas, Easter, Thanksgiving, or some other kind of celebration. I was, as always when I stayed there, in heaven. Now I have a theory that when we get up in the middle of the night, we do so with the memories of years of getting up in our own home and we know how to get the bathroom! For instance, in my home on Llandaff Road, I would get up from my bed, take four steps to the door, turn left, walk down the hall, take a right, walk into the bathroom, and sit on down. This same path at the Donatone house led me astray. To be exact, it led me to my Aunt Anne's favorite white wicker chair. Now, in my mind I had properly flushed the chair; it just didn't happen outside of my mind.

I awoke to screams of "Who the hell peed on the white wicker chair?" A funny feeling of familiarity overcame me, and I simultaneously realized that my pajamas should not have been wet. Within seconds, my cousins Carla and Anita were staring at me. "JANE!"

"What? It wasn't me! Why me?"

They demanded I get out of my sleeping bag to prove I had not wet myself. "No, I'm still tired. It's early."

"It's eleven, Jane. Get up."

Eventually, there was no avoiding the exposure and the guilt. The torment began.

A few months later we were all in New Jersey for a housewarming at my uncle's new condo. There are a couple of features of the typical condo that he should have taken into account before planning this party.

1. Condos are by their nature not vast mansions.

2. They hardly ever fit thirty-eight people comfortably, especially when two of them are in wheelchairs.

3. You should abort party plans if rain is forecast.

4. Seventeen children in one small room stuck there due to the rain, can lead to no good. In fact, it is a recipe for a terrible wicker-chair disaster.

So the storytelling began. First ghost stories, then the scariest story of them all, "remember when Jane peed on the white wicker chair?"

"Hahahahahhhhahahahhahhahhahahhahahahhahhahaha!"

All but one of the seventeen kids was laughing very vigorously. Guess who was not laughing?

So it went on and on, and finally, I didn't care that it was raining and went outside, where I could still hear the chortling inside. While outside the door I found out that the only funnier thing than hearing the story of my peeing on the white wicker chair was hearing it a second time. The third time causes hysteria, and the fourth time sent me on a mission to find a suitable place to injure myself and make them all feel terrible about laughing at me.

I started walking away from the condo/closet-warming, and soon I heard someone else come out.

My dad had joined me. I was crying, and he asked me what was wrong. I told him the story, and he just held my hand. "Well, let's go back inside; I think they'll knock it off now."

"You do?" I asked.

"Yeah, I think so," he said.

We went back in, and everyone was still laughing, I think I caught my mom snickering, but I decided to ignore that—too much turmoil already.

Something you should know about my dad and his place as Uncle Joe: he was loved and admired for his sense of humor, craziness, and kindness. "Hey," he announced. "All you people who are making fun of Jane. I have some news for you. Guess who the biggest bed wetter was that ever lived? ME! So who wants to make fun of Uncle Joe?"

Everyone was silent. One of my cousins asked, "Is that true, Uncle Joe?"

"Absolutely," he said.

My dad was heroic that day. Admitting a lack of control over his bladder in his youth may not sound like jumping-on-agrenade heroic, but to me, he jumped on my wet sleeping bag and the white wicker chair at the same time.

My dad was my savior on so many occasions that I can't even remember them all.

The kids stopped mocking me about the accident. At least, while we were at the party.

Over the next couple of months, comments came, some funnier than others. My brother Biggs went for the direct approach. "Hey, pee on any white wicker chairs today?"

My brother Pat was a bit more sneaky. "Hey, did you see that sign we just passed?"

Someone in the van would say, "No."

"Someone is selling stuff back there, big sale on white wicker chairs. Just one thing: there are yellow spots all over them."

"Ha ha ha ha ha," I would retort, using my best comeback.

Then Timmy would say, "Careful, you can pee when you laugh really hard. Are you sitting on anything white?"

It really was enough. I made a secret pact with myself to sneak into everyone's bed and pee at will. I never did it because even to me that is just too gross.

But that day my dad saved me. I could suffer my family's humiliating comments a million times over; it would all have been worth it for that wicker-induced valor that showed me how much he loved me.

Joe Baker, Father, Husband, Beer Drinker, Roofer, Pretend Bed Wetter...HERO!

CHAPTER 3

Cousin Carla

When I think of my childhood, I think of the fear and worry that was always below the surface. This is not to say that there was not a great deal of fun in the Baker house, because there was. But I felt I could not be responsible for two other people; I felt overwhelmed by the pressure. I would sit in the house and try to go through escape scenarios should the house catch on fire, if a nuclear mishap should occur in our kitchen, or any number of the potpourri of disasters I was able to conjure should take place. I made plans on how to get Pat and Dave out of the house or into the bomb shelter we did not have, or somewhere safe should the coming calamity occur on my watch. I was also certain a burglar/kidnapper would break into our house, and I went through every nook deciding where to hide.

FUN FACT: I picked my mom's closet, for it had both the deceptive depth to hide in and jelly beans and other candies my mother hid from us.

My family spent most holidays and vacations with my dad's side of the family. My mom's side was a never-ending string of bizarre characters doing strange things in New Jersey. To this day I honestly don't know how many cousins I have on my mom's side. We were always closest with my dad's sisters. My aunts Anne and Betty were great. Aunt Anne was bohemian; Aunt Betty was Bohemian Rhapsody, bohemian 2.0.

My aunt Betty did things like imply skinny-dipping had taken place in her presence. My Aunt Betty married a guy whom my father referred to as Uncle Asshole. We kids called him a most vile name that I am too polite to repeat (but it rhymed with Uncle Truck). When my Aunt Betty finally divorced the schmuck, she changed her name. This is where the true bohemian shows her face. She did not just change her name back to Betty Baker—how banal. No, my aunt took it up a notch, renaming herself the Countess Liz Von Becker. Why? I don't know, but it does lend her an air of mystery, doesn't it?

My Aunt Anne cursed, using horrifying words like "damn it" or "crap." She did crazy things like make oatmeal that was not instant. She did not go by any standard timekeeping system. When we had family events, we would eventually lie to Aunt Anne and tell her the function was three or four hours earlier than it was. This proved to work in getting her there before it was over. My aunt was someone I wanted to be like when I grew up. She always seemed smarter and more clever than all the other adults.

Her kids, my cousins, all went to public school. This confused me; when I was young I had assumed they were Catholic like us. There was a time in my life when I thought there were only two religions, Catholic and Public. This got cleared up pretty quickly when my brother Tim called me an idiot and explained.

The biggest thrill of my young life was staying overnight at the cousins. They lived in what we thought was the country on three acres. So pretty much the Forest. I thought they were hippies, and pretty cool. My cousin, whom I'll call Popcorn, had a drum set, and that was way cool. My other cousin, Popcorn 2, told me everything I was not ever supposed to know.

Once when I stayed at their house, Carla (whoops, I mean Popcorn 2) said, "So, I know something about your family that you don't."

I said, "Oh yeah? What?"

"I'm not allowed to tell you," she said. Statements like that make me want to run into a wall. Why taunt me? Naturally I wouldn't shut up until she said she would tell me.

"Okay, so, you have to swear you won't tell who told you … but Bake is your half brother, and your mom was married before she married your dad."

What a spin I was in. "Um, I think you are wrong on that. I would think that I would know that."

"It's true" was all she said. Now I had my theory: my aunt was married before she married my Uncle John, and Carla had two older siblings who were half siblings, and she just didn't want to feel alone, so she was making this up about my mom.

"Sure thing, Carla."

So when I returned home I went into my mother's room She was lying on her bed smoking a Raleigh cigarette and watching Match Game when I delicately put feelers out on the

Carla story. "Mom, Carla says you were married before and that Bake isn't really my brother."

My mother sat up and put her cigarette out. Then she lit another. "That Carla, she sure is beautiful, but not a brain in her head. Why did she tell you that?"

I assumed my mom was denying the story, "Yeah, I wondered that too, I guess she was just playing a joke on me ... right?"

My mother was not good at hiding a secret once it jumped out at her. "Well, Bake is your brother, but I was married before I married Dad."

"Ha ha, Mom, very funny." I guess she could see that I was not happy with this revelation, and so I decided to pretend it was still a joke. "Jane, I was married to a man named Jerry (she told me his last name but it started with a Z, and I just can't remember any word that starts with a Z). He died during the war. He got sick in Europe and came home and died. Bake was two years old."

"Okay, so Dad isn't Bake's father?" I asked.

"Well, Daddy is the only father that Bake knows. He doesn't remember his father."

Now I was not sure if I was part of a conspiracy or not. "So does Bake know this?"

"Yes, but nobody else does."

The next question I asked might make me seem a bit daft, but like I said, I was in a spin. "Does Dad know?"

"Jane, think about it. Bake was two. Yes, Daddy knows. He adopted Bake when we got married."

"Oh, okay." I felt a little better now, even though I felt bad for my dad, like maybe he didn't think he was my mom's first choice, but at least he knew, so I figured that if he was okay with that, I could be too.

I asked my mother if she had any pictures of this man who she married before my dad, and after closing her bedroom door she opened her closet and reached into the farthest-back part and pulled out a wedding album. This struck me as odd because I had always asked to see pictures of my parents' wedding but was always told that they were lost. So here was this album, full of pictures of a beautiful woman, my mother, and a very cute guy, her first husband. Many of these pictures I had seen before but none of the ones with Jerry in them. I had always assumed that these pictures were of my dad and mom's wedding, but now I knew the truth. I didn't like the looks of this guy, for no other reason than that he wasn't my dad, who actually was so much more handsome. For a few minutes I became acutely aware of how close I had come to not existing. My mother told me that I was not to tell my siblings about the other husband. Turned out that she worried that Pat and Dave might somehow think that it was my father who was responsible for their getting muscular dystrophy, since Bake had a different father and didn't get the disease. This of course makes no sense on several different levels. My parents had two more boys who did not get the disease. There is also the small fact that the disease is maternally X-linked. A father plays no role in the son's fate. Perhaps my mom did know that it all came down to her, and in keeping this secret she was actually keeping her feelings of guilt to herself. Whatever the intent, it did not last long, as my mother often said, "If Carla knows something, the world knows it." Carla told me many more things. In fact, I now realize that most of the things I didn't want to know about in life were told to me by Carla. But if you have to hear stuff you don't want to hear, you couldn't ask for a more beautiful, funny, or smart girl to hear it from.

CHAPTER 4

David

In the summer of 1977 we rented a house for two weeks with our cousins, the Donatones, in Avalon, New Jersey. Our cousins were a very good-looking bunch.

Walking along the beach with my cousin Carla made me feel quite invisible. Carla was only sixteen or seventeen but already probably close to six feet tall, with long blond hair. Quite frankly, she was beautiful gliding along the beach in her slightly present bikini. I was fourteen, probably close to five foot four, with short black hair. If I recall I was wearing a parka due to what I felt was a chill in the air during this unseasonably cold July. The Donatones were the beautiful people. We were the Addams Family. I found great joy in watching my brother Tim get a terrible sunburn on his huge, sheet-white belly while my Adonis cousin Alan just got tanner and better-looking. I got such joy because it took my mind off of the guys on the beach yelling "Hey, baby" at my cousin and "Hey, dork in the parka" to me.

This summer David was clearly getting much sicker. He was seventeen. He had gotten progressively weaker the past few years, and it became harder and harder for me to believe my fantasy that a cure would be found for his illness and that our family doctor, Dr. Burke, would stroll into our home and inject Pat and Dave with the cure and they would both just get up out of their wheelchairs and we would all cry and laugh and have a cinematic montage of happy. On July 13, I was lying in my bed in the room I was sharing with my younger sister and my cousins Carla and Anita. I was in that funny place between sleep and eavesdropping on conversation not intended for me. I heard Aunt Anne say to Carla, "David is very bad. Uncle Joe and Aunt Dolores might take him to the hospital."

I got out of bed and went downstairs. Everyone older than me was awake but sitting silently in the living room. I headed into the room where my brothers were staying, just off the living room, when one of my brothers said not to go in. I found my mother in the kitchen smoking a cigarette and looking horrible. She told me that she was catching up on the laundry. It was one o'clock in the morning. I told her I would go get the dirty clothes, which was my excuse for going into my brothers' room. When I entered the room, I saw my brother David on the bed in his underwear talking to my dad. My dad was crying, and David was saying things I didn't understand. Timmy was in the room in his underwear too, and you could see the fear in his eyes. David started saying that he wanted to be moved over. So Timmy moved him over. "More," David said, but Tim said, "Dave, you are on the edge, man." But David asked again to be moved further, so Timmy picked him up and held him off the bed over where he wanted to be. David was little more than skeletal now, and when I looked up at Timmy I saw tears flowing down his cheeks. When I think of my brother Tim today, that is the first image that comes to my mind; it's also the most beautiful. David then said, "Who is that over there?"

I said, "Dave, it's me Jane."

"Run, run to third, you can run to third."

I was confused and looked at my Dad, who explained, "We are in a baseball game every now and then, hon." David loved sports. When the Flyers won the Stanley Cup a couple of years earlier, I was afraid he was going to have a heart attack he was so excited. Phillies baseball, Flyers hockey, and Eagles football—he loved them all.

"Okay, I'll run, Dave."

"Did you make it?" he asked.

"Yeah, I did, and I stole home and we got a home run."

"Yes," he said, "we are winning."

When I took the clothes to my mother, she asked me if I thought David was okay. I was only fourteen, but I knew when someone was not okay.

I knew my mother knew David was not okay. So I said, "I think he's okay," 'cause I was fourteen and didn't want to break my mother's heart.

The next day my oldest brother came down from home with a pal in the Llanarch Fire Company ambulance. When they put David on the stretcher and hooked him up to some oxygen, I helped them put the tank on the stretcher next to David. "I'll see you soon, Dave," I said. I really thought I would.

When they took him out, I ran up the stairs, and my father followed me. I sat on the bed in the room crying, and my dad sat down next to me. "Are you okay, hon?" he said.

"Is David going to die dad?" I asked.

"Yeah Jane, he is." and he began to cry.

"Will he go to heaven?" I asked.

"Yes Jane, he will."

We then had a brief discussion about God and beliefs.

The next day I sat on the side porch of the shore rental with Pat and Timmy. From the porch we could see all the way down the main drag and I recognized my brother Mike's van from 40 blocks away. It's hard to miss a converted van with a huge drawing of the country on the side. My brother was strange and he had this painted on his van along with the inscription "country livin'." We lived in suburban Philly. I think the country livin must have been a drug reference of some kind.

"There's Bake's van." I said and Timmy and Pat looked for it. Timmy was lying on a wicker lounger and then rolled away from us. I looked at Pat and he had one tear coming down his face and all I could think was that I didn't know if I should wipe it away for him because he couldn't or if I shouldn't.

My parents got out of the van after it pulled into the drive. They were both wearing dark shades. As soon as they got out my older brother Bake took off. My aunt ran out to meet my parents and they all came into the house and out to the porch where we were. We were the only three kids home, the rest were sent to the beach by my Aunt.

My dad said, "David is dead." I was stunned by the harshness of the words, not "passed away," not "has died," but "is dead." My mother said that, "David went into a coma last night and then he died in the night." That's the only thing that was ever said about it and we watched as our other family members came in and were told that David had died.

When my only younger brother Biggs came home and heard, he ran out the back of the house. I followed him into the garage and found him sitting on an overturned canoe. He was sobbing and stopped to ask, "Why didn't anybody tell me he was going to die?"

We drove home later that night and I remember having never felt so lonely though I was in a van with eight other people. When we walked into the house I went to Pat and David's room and found David's side of the room empty. The company that supplied the hospital equipment, bed and oxygen had come and taken it all away. That night I slept on the floor where David's bed been had been; soon my cousin Jay joined me, then Biggs, then Joanne and finally Tim.

We were all, everyone but Bake and my parents, just being near each other. I don't know if we were all there protecting Pat from death, but I thought I was. I think I was also waiting should David come back. David did not come back and no one could protect Pat from death, but Pat made death work hard before it got him.

CHAPTER 5

Gun Safety

One day I was out front on our porch playing cards with my little brother Biggs when we heard my mother yelling from inside the house. It was not an "I'm hurt," or a "someone's in trouble," kind of yell. It was more of an "I have had enough!" yell. We felt safe in terms of not having heard our names mentioned. During some part of the rant I heard the word gun. I knew that my dad liked guns and that he probably had one or two. He had his office for the roofing company in the house, and that office had some lockable file cabinets in it, and I always assumed that he probably kept any extra beer, chewing tobacco, and/or guns he had in there. I was incorrect. A moment later my mother came out of the front door carrying at least eight guns. Some were pistols, some looked like fake cowboy guns, at least one was a shotgun, and there was something that looked perhaps German or Russian. My brother and I just stared, as kids are liable to do when looking at their angry mother holding many weapons. She looked at us. "Guns! Can you believe this? Guns!"

"Mom!" Pat called from his room. "Biggs, come get me! Mom, don't move."

Biggs went inside and brought Patrick out front onto the porch with us. "What?" my mother asked Patrick.

"Mom, what are you doing?"

"Oh, I'm teaching your father a lesson! That's what I'm doing!" she said.

"What are you going to do with the guns, Mom?" Pat asked.

"Your father wants guns in the house? Why just in the house, why not all around the house?" she said as she walked down the outside steps and dropped the guns into a pile on the grass.

"Mom, that's dangerous," Pat said.

"Dangerous? You think that's dangerous? I've told your father a hundred times if I found a gun not locked away, I would get rid of them. So there! Gone!"

"Well, technically, not really gone, they are lying on the grass," Pat said.

"They are out of the house!"

My mom stormed into the house, and we all just froze. By now all the kids from the neighborhood had gathered in the yard to look at the armed crazy lady. Then my father pulled up.

My dad always had a smile on his face when he came home, and today the smile didn't slide off his face until he saw the gun show.

"Jesus Christ, what the hell? Pat?"

"Mom was mad."

"No shit! What the hell? She's lost her goddamn mind."

Hearing her groom speaking, my mother flitted out to the porch, carrying her ashtray.

"Delores, are you out of your mind?"

"How many times did I tell you not to have guns in the house, Joe?"

"Delores, why would you put them on the lawn?"

"I told you I wanted them out of the house! They are out of the house!"

"They are in the goddamn yard, Delores!" My dad was sweating and shaky. "What if someone picked one up, Delores? What then?"

"Luckily you never loaded them!"

This led to my dad's surprise. "Jesus Christ Delores! Of course they are loaded!"

Which led to the third and last surprise. Surprise is what you feel when your mother drops and shatters her glass ashtray on the porch and runs inside the house.

One thing I always thought so sweet of my dad was that he would always explain away my mom's crazy with a little statement that made you know all would be okay.

Things like:

"Oh Jane, God only knows what's wrong with her."

"Oh, Jane, she has a lot on her mind."

"Oh, Jane, if murder was legal …"

"Oh Jane, you know I love that woman more than anything in this world."

"Oh Jane, I'm the luckiest bastard that ever lived."

"Oh, Jane, if I'm dead in the morning, your mother did it."

Delores and Joe circa 197*CRAZY*

CHAPTER 6

Learning to Drive with Bake

After turning sixteen, I was of course eager to get my driver's license. Although my father had no heart issues, this was his go-to excuse as to why he didn't teach any of us to drive. I had long ago chosen Timmy to teach me, but he'd gone and joined the stupid Navy just to spite me. So I found myself at the mercy of Bake.

Let me give you a slice of Bake so you can understand my apprehension. Have you ever heard of the band The Tubes? I have. Bake came home one day from the store having recently purchased an album by The Tubes. I couldn't tell you the name of that album, but I can tell you that I hated it. I loved "Hello, Dolly!" and "West Side Story," and like every girl my age, I sang "Annie" tunes till my throat bled. Unlike most girls, I was also in love with Andrea McArdle, the first Annie. Bake played a song from this Tubes album. It hurt my soul. "You like it?" he asked.

"It's not really the kind of music I like," I said.

"Nah, you didn't even listen, I'll play it again." He did and I did listen and I still hated it. "I don't like it, Bake," I told him.

"Listen to the next song. You'll really like the next song." He played the next song. I hated it.

"I don't like it Bake," I said.

"Well, this is disappointing, I figured you would like it because I thought you had good taste in music."

What the hell? "Just because I don't like the music you like doesn't mean I have bad taste in music, Bake," I declared, proud of my ability to stand up to his male music privilege and his stubborn music pushing.

"Yes, it does, " he replied.

"No it does not!" I countered.

"Actually, it does. Your taste in music officially sucks, no second chances, no take backs, you can't listen to my album."

For someone as remarkably intelligent as my brother Bake was, his concept of punishing someone whose opinion differed from his was asinine.

"So you have an album I hate and I can't listen to it? Boy, you got me, I'm so burned!" I said.

"Yeah, I know, fine. I'll let you hear one more song," he said.

I realized that I just had to lie and tell him I liked the Tubes or die from the tunes eating at my brain. He played another song. I loved it, I loved it so much, it was the best song I ever heard, could he put it on a cassette for me? I often wondered if he was that removed from reality to think I meant any of that or if he was just stoned or drunk. All seemed equally likely. So I liked a Tubes song and could leave unharmed. "Thanks, I can't wait for the cassette," I said, ending the conversation.

"Yeah, I knew you would like it," he added. He had that thing where you had to have the last word in an argument. I think it's called being an ass.

So - time to learn to drive. Bake was a volunteer fireman. Our firehouse was so close that if he jogged, he could easily have made it there in time to make a call. However, if you jog, nobody gets to see you driving with a cool light on your roof. Bake was obsessed with fire safety and, by extension, scaring the shit out of me while teaching me to drive. Bake drove us to the fire-training grounds and lectured me on the way. "Are you prepared for the responsibility of being a driver?" he inquired.

"I don't know ... I guess so," I said.

"I can turn around now and we can do this when you are prepared for the responsibility. This is not a game and a car is not a toy."

When your driver's license is held in the balance, you find yourself willing to acquiesce to even the stupidest statements. "Don't turn around, I know it's not a toy."

This was just enough begging to satiate his crazy ego and, according to him, "superior teaching ability." We arrived at the fire grounds, and he turned off the van.

We got out, and I walked over to get into the driver's seat. Prematurely.

"Whoa, slow down. Let's go over a few things. First, you need to acknowledge that from the second you get in that driver's seat you control a vehicle of death," he stated.

"What the hell, Bake, I just want to learn to drive. Jesus," I said, immediately aware that I had probably said the wrong thing. I was correct. For the next half hour he recounted all the stories he could think of where he had been on an ambulance call and what the wreckage and deceased look like and his opinion of what the drivers had done to cause their own demise. Some reasons were: Defensive Driving, Offensive Driving, Overly Cautious Driving, Aggressive Driving, Passive Driving, Passive-Aggressive Driving, Drunk Driving, and DWF. Of course asking what DWF meant was silly, as I should have guessed it was a hilarious acronym for Driving While Female. Let the hysterical laughing begin! I sure did laugh! God, that's funny stuff.

While the lecture went on, Bake took pylons from the training tower and set them up around the parking lot. Finally I was going to drive a car…backwards…through pylons. I asked

Bake if starting out going forward without pylons might be a better first step. He did not think so. My first attempt was less than perfect. I hit every pylon, crushing them all and mysteriously making one disappear. I found this pretty amusing. Mr. Grim Reaper did not. "Get out of the driver's seat!" he insisted.

"Bake, I never drove before, Jesus, they're just pylons," I whined.

"Pylons? No, not pylons, my friend, each pylon represented a person. A person you just murdered. A person who will not go home to their family tonight, a person who will not get married, not have children, a person too young to die," Bake said, clearly headed for the deep end.

"Bake, that last pylon was elderly and had no family, was married, had several kids, they all grew up and went to college, it's fine," I said, highly amused by myself. "Ha ha ha, murderer. Lesson is over. Get the pylons and put them in the tower. Time to go home," said the overly dramatic brother.

"Oh come on!" I said. "You are not going to stop teaching me because I made a joke!"

"No, that's just all the time we have today."

"What the hell, I drove for fifteen seconds, Bake!" I was furious.

"Learning to drive is not a race; we will take our time. Also, you killed eight people in fifteen seconds. I think that's enough carnage for one day."

Six months later my brother Timmy came home from the Navy for a week and I learned to drive and got my license. I flipped Bake the bird every time I saw him when I was driving. Still do.

Tim Baker, Competent Driving Instructor and Navy Man.

CHAPTER 7

The Poconos

Our family vacations were normally spent at the shore. (In the Philadelphia area, this means the New Jersey Shore).

Around 1975, my mom and dad were trying to think of something that would be more fun for Pat and Dave as the beach was a bit of a bitch for them. Wheelchairs sink in the sand.

They never complained, and we did have lots of fun at the arcades and boardwalks, and we all enjoyed enormous amounts of food. Shore food was even better than food at home! My father used to say if we were acting up in the van; then he could turn around and sit in the backyard for two weeks and drink his beer. Apparently shore beer was no better than Havertown beer.

Along came someone who knew someone who had a house in the Pocono Mountains that was perfect for us. A very large house with a ramp, paved roads, many rooms, bedrooms on the ground floor, a lake nearby. So perfect.

We were going to the Poconos! Very exciting.

My father's only brother, our "bachelor" uncle, was coming with us, and it was decided that my sister Joanne and I would ride the four hours with him. Everyone else was riding in the van my parents had rented but which had not arrived yet. All of us kids waited outside with our bags and excitement when a cargo van pulled up and a man, looking like he drove a cargo van got out.

My father came out of the house looking like a mash-up of confusion and anger.

Cargo man and my dad had a brief discussion, of which we heard only the louder highlights. Some that had real gusto were "You're a chicken's ass!" and "You said you were transporting wheelchairs, buddy!"

Clearly there had been a misunderstanding as to the nature of the wheelchairs and the fact that they were only two and were indeed occupied. Some hours later a different van appeared one with windows and seats. One that wouldn't look like my dad was a wheelchair wholesaler.

Packed up and ready to go, we hit the very long boring road to our dream vacation house.

A few things you should know about my Uncle, Bachelor. Persnickety is a word that comes to mind. Flamboyant, pesky, annoying, and shithead are others. Uncle Bachelor had many irritating habits. One was that he was a hyper honker. You didn't need to do anything wrong while driving to earn a honk from him. He honked randomly. I think I suffered PTSD for a few weeks after that trip. He honked at everyone, and then he commented on his or her real or perceived shortcomings.

For example, if someone was going too slow in the right lane, where you are allowed to go slower = HONK and "Well, hello, grandmother, go home and get dinner and get off the road—some of us are driving!"

Someone having the gall to drink a beverage while driving = HONK and "This is a highway, not a café in France! Drive or get off the road."

CB radios were big in those years. Talk on one = HONK and "Hello 'good buddy,' stop chatting with your friends and drive or get off the road."

Parents who looked like they were having some difficulty with their unruly children= HONK and "Control those kids before they cause a pile-up of ungodly carnage."

My parents did not appreciate his honking at them. Joanne and I waved like it was a friendly honk. One of the boys flipped us the bird. I don't think my uncle saw that or God knows what kind of honking frenzy would have ensued.

What felt like many days later but was only hours later, we arrived and pulled up next to the rental van. I'll never forget the image of my mother beating the shit out of the front of the van with her purse. "Why? Why would someone do this? What is wrong with people? Dear God, why?"

Expecting to see my family slaughtered by the mystery ax murderer of the mountain, I was surprised to see everyone alive and well. My father was trying to console her. "Let's go inside, Delores, it might not be that bad."

I looked at the cabin. It was that bad. Unless it was like in a dream when you open the door and it became amazingly bigger inside than it appeared from outside.

The driveway was not paved; it was in fact what you might do to a driveway if someone told you to make it impossible to traverse in wheelchairs. It was not pebbles; it was large rocks. The driveway led up to a very quaint little cabin—perhaps today it would be called a "tiny house." There were twelve of us if you counted.

Uncle Bachelor, and we counted him as three people, all assholes.

Pat and Dave were carried in their wheelchairs into the closet house, and we took a tour.

One bedroom downstairs, tiny, one small bed. Wheelchair-accessible? Absolutely not. One bathroom, no door—well done! There was a large sitting room (see photo).

We sat. Obviously, we could not stay here. As we sat around waiting for my parents to come up with a plan, it occurred to us that we saw only one bedroom. There was supposed to be a second floor.

Biggs and I set out to find it. Having never accessed another floor by pulling on a string, it was odd for us to find that a stairway could come down from the ceiling if you pulled on a string. We pulled and a stairway did come down, halfway. My dad boosted us up to get us high enough to climb the stairs and check out the bedrooms upstairs. It did not take long. There were five beds, or I should say mattresses, kept off the ground by the innovative use of tires as bed frames. There was also a pile of Playboy and Time magazines. "The News and Nudies Collection," I liked to call it. We got down off the partial stairs and closed that floor off. My father had headed out with a mission to find us a solution, and a few hours later we were back in the vehicles headed to the Holiday Inn.

Later in life my father told me that he had driven to the local hotel in a panic because he believed in cash, not checks, and certainly not credit cards and was sure we would be stranded at the rental house. He said that he just told the manager of the hotel that he was an honest man, he didn't have credit cards, but he would leave the man his business card, and he would send a check for payment when he got back home. He didn't tell me if he mentioned that my mother was on the verge, but I definitely would have added that for good measure. The manager let us stay at the hotel, and we had a great time.

I have many pictures from that vacation, the only one we ever spent in the Poconos.

CHAPTER 8

My Sister Joanne

(Joanne and me. Please note subtle wallpaper of the 70's-pic)

Once a princess is born unto a family, thou shalt cease procreating, and this is why my parents stopped populating the church when Joanne was born. I only have one sister; her name is Joanne. My two sons call her Aunt Joanne. Her husband calls her "wife." Her daughter calls her "Mom." I have often said that Joanne is the daughter my mother always wanted, which is to clearly say that I was not. My dad always loved me and was amused by my tomfoolery whereas my mother was just disappointed. My sister liked all things girly, dresses and dolls and sparkles, She did not, however, like girls, a distinct difference between us.

My sister is painfully straight, so straight that it's like she was born that way or something. God only knows what happened to her. Maybe a bad experience with a woman or she was just too hideous to get a girl. Whatever the reason, she has remained resolutely heterosexual. This girl is so straight that when we went to the Tower Theater to see k.d. lang live in concert, although ever other human in the theater was plotting to give up their freedom for a night with k.d., my sister said, "She has a good voice." A good voice. Case closed, she is straighter than anyone ever needed to be. But, live and let live I say!

My sister has been a great amusement to me in life. Throughout our lives I have taken every opportunity to embarrass, frustrate or just infuriate her.

Here are only a few examples of how I have probably messed with her mental health. Most of the events here have been told to my kids at bedtime. That they will remember these as bedtime stories is both epically satisfying and tragically cruel.

Although I think it would be nice if the harassment had stopped when we became adults, the truth is it did not. As recently as last year I called her at work to remind her that it's always possible I will strike unannounced. Joanne has worked for twenty years or more at an eye doctor's office. She has had the most awesome and supportive boss a person could ask for. Her co-workers, however, are a bit thin skinned if you ask me.

Throughout these twenty years that she has been there, I have made random calls to her office trying to trick her into thinking there was a person on the phone with a legitimate problem. The first time I called I was playing it cool, not too big a problem, but a big enough one to get her concerned.

The call went something like this:

Joanne: Really Cool Eye Center, this is Joanne.

Jane: I'm sorry, what is your name?

Joanne: Joanne, can I help you?

Jane: Yes, I hope you can. I can't decide if I need to see a doctor right away or if it can wait til tomorrow; I know it's late in the day, so you probably could not squeeze me in!

Joanne: OK, well are you a patient of ours?

Jane: Not yet.

Joanne: Oh, well, what is the problem you are having?

Jane: It's my eye.

Joanne: Yes, that makes sense. What is wrong with your eye?

Jane: Well it fell out.

Joanne: What?

Jane: Fell right out, 'bout a half hour ago.

Joanne: I don't understand. I'm sorry, what are you saying?

Jane: I should explain, I was vacuuming and somehow tripped, and the vacuum got stuck on my eye and pulled it right out.

Joanne: Do you have a glass eye?

Jane: I wish! That would be much less bloody.

Joanne: Are you saying your eye is out of its eye socket, and it's a real eye?

Jane: 100% real eye, yes, hanging out. What do you think I should do?

Joanne: You need to go to the ER right now.

Jane: It can't wait until tomorrow?

Then there was a pause. A couple of beats of silence and then she said.

Joanne: Jane is this you?

Jane: Yeah.

Joanne: You bitch! I'm having a heart attack here! Damn it.

Jane: But you think I should go to the ER?

Joanne: I hate you. (Hangs up)

The above dialog is what I mean by my little sister being a bit of a baby. No need for rudeness! So she hung up on me. I didn't give up, and I have lots of voices, so I waited for a few months and called back as an elderly woman. If someone other than Joanne answered, I would just say, "Wrong number" and call back until I got Joanne.

Call number 2.

Elderly woman and Joanne:

Joanne: Really Cool Eye Center, this is Joanne.

Jane: Hi Joanne this is Mrs. Baxter. I was in last week, and I think I left something in the office.

Joanne: Mrs. Baxter? Can I get your first name and I can look you up in the system?

Jane: I don't think that's needed, I just want to know if anyone turned in my things.

Joanne: OK, I usually remember all our patients and I'm drawing a blank, I'm sorry.

Jane: That's fine, do you have a lost and found?

Joanne: Not really but anything anyone found would have been given to the front desk so I can check. What is it that you forgot?

Jane: I had a beige bag, like a large bag, and there were some items in it. Do you have a pencil? I'll give you a list.

Joanne: I don't think I need a list I'll look for the bag how's that?

Jane: But items could have fallen out.

Joanne: Ok. I have a pencil, go ahead…

Jane: Ok, first the bag.

Joanne: Beige bag, got it.

Jane: One P&B sandwich.

Joanne: Ok. Probably not good anymore!

Jane: We'll see.

Joanne: Ok. Go on.

Jane: December, January and February editions of Time, Life and Playgirl magazine.

Joanne: Oh. Ok.

Jane: As you know, I'm blind, so they are the braille editions.

Joanne: Braille? I did not know Playgirl had a braille edition.

Jane: Oh it sure does! You should read it.

Joanne: I just might. Was there anything else?

Jane: Oh, yes, my car keys.

Joanne: Didn't you just say you were blind?

Jane: I'm not that blind.

Joanne: I'm pretty sure any level of blind means you can't drive. Let me look you up! What's your first name?

Jane: Jane.

Joanne: You bitch. (Hung up)

So sensitive she was. The next call was more direct.

<u>Call number 3.</u>

Joanne: Really Cool Eye Center, this is Joanne.

Jane: Dear god help me my eye is infected with noodles!

Joanne: Bitch (Hung up)

I waited for a few more years and called back, this time as a nice Italian fella.

<u>Call number 4.</u>

Joanne: Really Cool Eye Center, this is Joanne.

Jane: Eh, yeah, problem, are your eyes supposed to bleed?

Joanne: Jane?

Jane: Yeah.

(Hung up)

These phone calls were par for what she expected from me. In our young adulthood this systematic unnecessary provocation of Joanne's person began innocently enough. One day we were going through a drive thru and Joanne was driving. We were just about at the order microphone, and I sneezed. I admit to having a troubling sneeze, but she whipped her head around at me and said, "Don't embarrass me." I was so offended! "What are you saying, you think I would embarrass you? God..."

Then we pulled up to the microphone.

Wendy's Employee: Welcome to Wendy's can I take your order?

Joanne: Yes, can I...

This was when I chose my moment to yell.

Jane: PLEASE ASK THAT YOU FREE WENDY!

My sister looked over at me with such rage.

Wendy's Employee: I'm sorry, what did you say?

Joanne: Nothing, Can I have...

Jane: ONE GOOD REASON YOU WON'T FREE WENDY!

Wendy's Employee: Are you just going to be a jerk or did you want to order something?

Joanne: I'm sorry, my sister is an idiot, and she won't shut up. Can I have a frosty, chocolate and some fries?

Wendy's Employee: Large or small frosty?

Joanne looked at me, and I knew that if I said anything else, I was going to be in trouble.

Joanne: Large frosty, medium fries please.

Wendy's Employee: Sure, pull up to the window.

Joanne rolled up the window and turned to me.

Joanne: Get out of my car!

Jane: Ok. (I got out)

Joanne: What the hell are you doing?

Jane: I'm getting out of your car. I'll just walk around to the front and you can pick me up there. Give you a second to calm down.

Joanne: WAIT, she'll think it was all me, you need to get in the car!

Jane: No I don't.

Joanne: Get in the car.

Jane: Nope.

So I closed the door and walked to the front of the restaurant and watched as she pulled up to the window. I had a perfect view of the girl at the window and Joanne. I don't know who looked more confused, but it was a beautiful show of awkward. I could tell Joanne wanted to explain, but there is also something that tells you when you are just going to dig yourself deeper. Joanne was always good at just shutting up. She pulled up a second later with her Frosty and fries. And no, she would not share.

The next time we went to a drive through she made me swear I wouldn't say a word and since I was hungry and she was buying I promised not to talk, and she promised to get me whatever she got herself. Luckily I didn't need to say anything to embarrass her this time. Joanne loved her music and always had it on really loud. She stopped singing along to order, but her volume was pretty high.

Joanne: Hi, can I have two vanilla shakes and two fries?

Burger King Girl: Ma'am, you don't need to yell?

Joanne: Oh gosh, I'm sorry.

Burger King Girl: You are still yelling!

Joanne: I'm sorry!

Burger King Girl: Just pull up to the window, God!

Joanne looked at me and begged me to tell her it wasn't her fault; she wasn't screaming. I told her it was clearly not her fault and that the girl at the window was nuts.

Then we pulled up to the window, and Joanne tried to whisper, not anything I had ever heard her do up to this point.

Joanne: Hi. Sorry if you thought I was yelling, my sister is here, and she said that I wasn't, maybe it's your microphone system. Joanne looked over to me, and the girl leaned down so she could see me in the car. I had made myself cry and had tears streaming down my face when I looked at the girl, hands on my ears. "Please make her stop!" The girl looked at me with empathy in her eyes as Joanne lost her shit.

"No, she is full of shit! Damn it." We got our food, and again she did not share.

The next time we went to a drive through I gave her a choice, she could play along with me or suffer. She chose wisely and while she ordered I barked very loudly for the entire time. Joanne added a "Shhhhh Fritz, stop barking!" This added to the believability of our scene. When we pulled up, you could see the girl was looking for a dog in the car.

McDonalds Girl: I heard your dog he sounds so cute.

Joanne: What?

McDonalds Girl: Your dog.

Joanne: What dog?

McDonalds Girl: Oh, I'm sorry.

Joanne: Are you ok?

McDonalds Girl: Yeah, here's your food.

We pulled out of the lot and laughed, and I got to eat.

Stores, in general, were not a good place for Joanne to go into with me. The worst thing I ever did to her that put her in real danger of being arrested was in a Burlington Coat Factory store. They had real leather coats and some fur jackets before the time PETA would shoot you for owning fur. Other than going into a store with me in the first place, the next biggest mistake Joanne made was letting us split up and shop separately. I only went a few aisles over and watched her try on some jackets. Then she strolled past a display of jewelry. The fun thing about jewelry is that it's small enough to fit into your purse in the event you are a thief. I was not a thief. But my sister, she was not either. None of this mattered to me. I was not about to abandon my sister just because she was making a mistake. No, not me, I was going to be there to help her.

Jane loving sister: "Joanne, my sister, put that back."

Joanne horrified: "What? I don't have anything!"

Now we clearly had the attention of store security and a guard tried to look casual as he came closer.

Jane: "Joanne, shoplifting is stealing!"

Joanne: "Jane, I swear! Stop it!"

Jane: "Me stop it? How about you stop stealing from stores in the mall?"

Joanne looked right at the security officer.

Joanne: "Look, Sir, this is my sister, she's an idiot, and she is pretending."

The security guard looked at me and raised his eyebrows.

Jane: "I wish I was pretending. She's ruining her life. We've tried everything."

Joanne: "Stop it! Tell them right now you are lying or I'll kill you!"

Jane: "Well that is a violent threat! Officer, you should probably take her in, for my safety."

Joanne: "You ass!"

The security guard walked over to Joanne and very kindly said, "Do you have anything from the store in your bag Miss?"

Joanne: "No, would you like to look?"

The guard said that was okay; he didn't need to look.

Joanne: "Thank you, you have no idea how horrible my sister is."

Security Guard: "I think I have an idea."

Joanne: "Thank you, we'll leave now."

Security Guard: "That's a good idea."

We left the store, and Joanne went right to her car and told me to walk home. It was miles, and I didn't like to walk, at all. So I climbed on her car and told her I would never do anything like that again if she let me ride home with her. She let me in the car but it wasn't the smartest move, she knew I lied when faced with the prospect of having to walk somewhere.

Joanne and I have always agreed on some things, like she is more like an older sister than me. She has always been the pretty one. She has suffered because I'm her sister. We have a great time when we are together. I know she loves me and I do so love my sister.

CHAPTER 9

Can forgive, hard to forget.

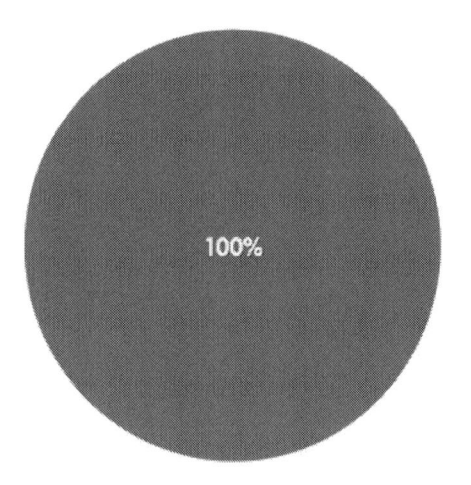

● percentage I hated this conversation

In 1986, months after Patrick had died, I was preparing to work at Summer Stage, a summer theater program that I had attended since I was thirteen. I had taught there before and was excited to do something fun again. I was preparing for classes when my father and I had an exchange that took me a while to sort through. This is how it played out in my head, between the two halves of my brain.

Yin: Go over it again.

Yang: OK, I was sitting in the den, writing my lesson plans for this summer…

Yin: OK…

Yang: …and Dad walks in, and I could tell he was smashed.

Yin: How?

Yang: He slurs and

Yin: …gets really funny.

Yang: Well, he used to, but he's been such an angry drunk since.

Yin: Since?

Yang: Since Pat died. I guess he's pissed off at the world.

Yin: Can't blame him…it's only been three months since his son died.

Yang: It's only been three months since my brother died.

Yin: It's different.

Yang: I don't believe in comparative pain. Pain is pain.

Yin: Well you have never been a parent.

Yang: I know that I'm just saying that I know this is the most devastating thing he has ever gone through, first David and now Patrick. "You shouldn't bury your children; they should bury you." Dad has said that a million times...and he's right...I just wonder sometimes if he and mom have ever thought, even for a second, that we might have needed their help dealing with this...for god's sake they were our brothers.

Yin: Ok, ok...back to what happened...

Yang: I was working on my lesson plans, and he was bitching at me that I shouldn't have taken the job and that I was wasting my education, and he was just getting madder and madder at me.

Yin: You could see he was getting mad?

Yang: Yeah, that's when I picked up my stuff and started to go up to bed.

Yin: And...

Yang: And he stopped me, and he started repeating over and over, "You know what I wish? You know what I wish? Do you?"

Yin: That is when you told him to think before he said something stupid?

Yang: Yeah.

Yin: Then what?

Yang: He was just looking at me, so I said, "Dad, open your wallet." When he did, I asked him "how many of my letters do you have in there?"

Yin: And he said...

Yang: Seven

Yin: All seven?

Yang: Yep, so I just said asked him what they were, and he just shrugged, like they were nothing. "Those are notes I have written to you since I was ten years old and they are filled with how much I love you and admire you and want to be like you."

Yin: And he said?

Yang: Nothing.

Yin: Nothing?

Yang: Nope. Then a couple of seconds later he started back with "You know what I wish? You know what I wish?" So I said, "What Dad, what do you wish?" I was thinking he was going to say that he wished I wasn't gay or that he wished he could stop missing Pat and Dave so much.

Yin: You already forgave him for this didn't you?

Yang: Of course, the man just buried his son. He's lost.

Yin: And you are queer.

Yang: Yes.

Yin: And that hurt him.

Yang: Yes, but I didn't want it to, I tried so hard not to hurt him. God, why would I want to hurt him; he is my idol…he was my idol.

Yin: Fine…so you knew he was going to say something about your being gay?

Yang: Yes, but he didn't.

Yin: What did he say?

Yang: He said, "I wish you had died instead of Patrick."

Yin: Oh…what did you do?

Yang: I said, "right now, so do I."

CHAPTER 10

Delores

My mother was a saint; ask my Dad and many others. To me my mother was many things: not all saintly, not all bad. I think that she loved me, perhaps even liked me, but not always. I have often wondered when staring at my children and being overwhelmed with wonder and love and gratitude if she ever looked at me in that way. I was her first daughter after four boys. She knew what she wanted her daughter to be like. I disappointed regularly. I hated girly clothes and girly things…found out later I did like girls! Luckily I was her first daughter and the second came and saved my mother's plan for the perfect girl. My sister loved and loves all things girly…but not girls. My mother had in my sister everything she wanted in a daughter. She had in me, everything else.

In September of 2002, my mother passed away. Or as she would have said, "Went to her heavenly reward." Nearly two years after my oldest son came into the world my mother was about to leave it.

In mid-2001 my mother became quite ill while on a trip with my father. An x-ray showed she had a very large tumor in her lung.

I got the news that my mother had cancer on my cell phone as Sharon, Sam and I were going into a Target store. I love Target stores and for me they were comforting…I don't know why. When I was a child and a movie scared me or my friends, we would all say, "Think of Disneyland, nothing bad happens there." This sometimes worked. As an adult, I had that feeling about Target, and it was almost surreal that I was told that my mother had Cancer when I was going into Target…only good things happen in Target! So now in addition to my mom having Cancer, Target was ruined for me as well. My experience with sick people in my family up until this time was that people got sick, got worse, and died. This was no different. My Mom went through chemo, radiation and I wonder if it was a good idea—it seemed to make things worse and cause more pain. I wonder if she had not gone the chemo and radiation route would she have lived more fully in her last months? Who is to say? I don't know what I would do; hope I never find out.

When I traveled to PA to visit my mom from Ohio, my mother expressed some fears that shocked me a bit. I had always assumed that my Mom and Dad would not fear death so much because of their sons already having gone before them. I also assumed that my Mother went to church every week because she had faith. I now wonder if she had hope, not faith. I have hope, but not faith. She also seemed very unsure of her place in an afterlife. She doubted her qualifications for heaven…this saddened me. I am not sure what happens after we die but what I am sure of it that is tragic to me when someone is so sure there is a heaven yet they think they might not get in. What annoys me about so many religions is the mere idea that a god or gods could be so cruel as to create impossible situations and punish people for trying their best to get through it. I sometimes ponder the possibility of there being a less than perfect resort heaven reserved somewhere for the mean and rotten and other people of that ilk. I have a friend from college who would kiss me on the lips for using the word "ilk." Pay up Penny!

In August 2002, I flew from Ohio to Philly because my mom was in the hospital. I think she had fallen or something like that, but I felt I needed to be near her. When I arrived at the hospital room, my father was sitting in a chair watching CNN. My mother was sleeping. It had been almost a year since the attacks, and the coverage on the news was all about the terrorists and GW's plan to bring them to justice. Bush always seemed to me to be stressing certain words when he talked about JUSTICE that made me think that perhaps George thought there was a physical place called Justice.

Anyhow, my Father is a big Republican and we have had some interesting talks about that. I'm always sure I am right, and he is always sure I am a "God Damn Bleeding Liberal Heart."

He was talking to the TV which was not unusual at all, "God Damn terrorists, they ought to line them all up and shoot them or blow their whole country up or…" I interrupted him from the doorway "I'm pretty sure they died in the planes Dad." He turned around and said, "You know what I mean, how are you hun?" and gave me a kiss. It was this dichotomy that I always loved about my dad; he was able to speak of murderous revenge and his love for his children in the same breath.

We talked for a bit before my mom woke up and my dad headed home to take care of some business now that I was with my mother. My mother and I made small talk for a while; I talked about Sam and Sharon and a job interview I had gone to in Vermont. I could tell my mom was glad I was there and excited to hear about things that could distract her from her fears. After a couple of hours, I remembered I had brought along a little photo book of our trip to Vermont with many cute pictures of her 8th grandchild Samuel Joseph. I may be biased since I birthed him, but I honestly think he was the cutest baby in the history of the world. Honestly. So I showed my mom these photos of Sam in his stroller in Vermont. Sam with his stuffed lamb named Putney Baa Baa. Sam in the hotel we stayed at in Vermont. Sam at the school I interviewed at in Vermont.

As I was telling my Mom about the job and the school and how beautiful it was in Vermont when Kay McCormack entered the room. Kay had been a close and dear friend of my mother for maybe forty years.

"Hello Mary Jane, did you fly in from Columbus?" I turned to her and gave her a hug and told her that I had flown in a few hours ago and was staying for several days. "Who is that beautiful boy in the pictures?" She asked. (Note "beautiful"…unsolicited opinion!)

"It's Sam, Mrs. McCormack!"

I realized by her expression that she had no idea who I was talking about. I looked at my mother who was looking suddenly guilty and angry and curiously interested in her blanket. She had that skill.

I turned back to Mrs. McCormack and said, "Sam is my son Mrs. McCormack, and he's one-and-a-half years old now."

"Don't be silly, you don't have a son Mary Jane!" she replied.

It was pretty clear in the few seconds of silence that Kay realized that as funny as it might have been to feign motherhood that I was not kidding, and my mother realized that she had been caught in her betrayal of her daughter.

My mother tried valiantly, "Oh Kay! I told you about Sammy. Jane and her friend Sharon…her friend…and Jane had Sam in October 2000, I told you that Kay!"

"You certainly did not Dolores; I would have remembered…"

I read somewhere that it's never considered good form to have a display of fisticuffs with a woman who has cancer and Kay could get riled up so I thought I should cool things down. "Oh, Mom, I'm sure you did tell her and Mrs. McCormack you probably didn't realize she meant another grandchild since she has so many!"

So Kay stayed for a while visiting with my mother, and I went for a cup of coffee. In the elevator back up from the café to my mom's floor a kind looking hospital volunteer asked if I was visiting family. "Yes, my mother."

"Do you live around here?" she inquired.

"Not anymore, I live in Ohio" I replied.

"Well, I'm sure your mother is very happy that you came so far to see her."

It was at that point that I realized that I don't always let my emotions out when I am hurt and might perhaps possibly take it out, on innocent bystanders.

"Actually," I told this poor trapped woman, "I just found out that my dear mother is so ashamed of me that she didn't even tell one of her closest friends that I have a son. He's beautiful, and he's the most wonderful thing I've ever been connected to and she didn't even tell her friend that he exists."

"Oh that must have been a mistake, I can't think why someone would do that…"

"Oh, I think I know…I'm gay, and I had the baby by an anonymous donor with my lesbian partner, I think maybe that's why."

The woman just muttered "Oh my," and stared at the elevator display. I can only imagine she was hoping for the elevator to move faster or for death to come soon.

Shockingly she got off at the next floor; she hadn't even pushed the button for that floor, but others were getting on, so fate was on her side.

"Nice talking to you…" I said

"Oh my." she muttered.

When I returned to my mother's room Kay was getting her coat on.

"You take care Mary Jane and give that boy a big squeeze; he's a cutie." Kay said on her way out.

I looked at my mom, and it pained me to see her struggling with what to say, but I waited.

"Oh Jane!" she said, sounding exasperated that she should have to explain herself. "I didn't tell Kay because, you know that she has a mouth! She would have told everyone."

I stood stunned, "Would that have been bad Mom?"

"For me… living here… in my town, yes it would have. I decide who knows," she said.

"I see." I said.

"Oh don't you dare get angry about this. You have no idea…" she was going to go on her tangent about how difficult it was for her to have a gay child…so I cut her off.

"I'm not angry Mom."

"Then what are you?" she asked defensively.

"I am hurt and sad." I said

"Oh great," was all she said.

"I love you mom, but I don't like you right now." I said.

"Fine!" she said.

"Fine," I said back.

Then she pointed to her closet in the corner. "Now get my wallet from my pocketbook, I saw a cute little doctors outfit I want you to get for Sammy from me."

My mother is gone, but I still have that cute little doctor's outfit.

Part Two

Friends / Skoolin

CHAPTER 11

Summer Stage

When I was fifteen, I joined the Upper Darby Summer Stage theater program for kids. I had finally arrived at the place I didn't know I was looking for. The first two people I remember meeting there were Tom and Kevin. I was taking an improv class with Bob Babish, and these two boys were in the class. I immediately liked both Tom and Kevin, and I found out later that Kevin immediately disliked me. I had a bit of a 'volume and being an obnoxious girl' issue back in those days. I also had at that time an inability to understand why someone might not like me. It's embarrassing to say that I still don't care for it when someone doesn't like me. My approach to hearing that Kevin didn't like me was different than it would be today, I hope. I said something obnoxious like, "So you think I'm obnoxious?"

You leave a person very little choice but to lie when you ambush them like that. "No, I didn't say that, who said I said that?" was Kevin's sad reply. It was the teacher who had said that, and he was in the room, so I said, "Bob said that."

Bob was a fabulous teacher, a wonderful guy, and a bit mischievous. I think he got a bit of a kick out seeing our friendships evolve or dissolve. Mischievous I tell you! Bob introduced me to Improvisation and for that I will always be in his debt.

Kevin looked at me with caution and looked at Bob with anger. "Bob, how could you say that?"

"Well Kevin, it is what you said, maybe you could tell Jane what it is that she is doing that annoys you?"

Kevin then made a noise I would become very familiar with. It was a sort of angry-whimper-frustrated-trapped animal sound. If I had to spell it phonetically, it might be "eeee-shas-fwaar-thrart."

I felt terrible that I had made a human being make that sound, and so I just said, "It's okay Kevin, I am obnoxious and loud, you'll get used to me, and we'll be great friends."

I wasn't really sure that would happen but thank god it did.

When I met Tom, it was like I had met my better-looking identical twin who happened to be a boy and much smarter and funnier than I. I fell in love with him completely. It was not until we were older that Tom would be aptly labeled "scathing," but he deserved the title from day one. Tom was the first person I ever remember making me belly laugh, and then painfully describing the vastness of that belly. Tom used to say that I had the whole world in my belly. If I had not found his delivery and his wit so killer I might have been offended but I did, so I wasn't. Later in our lives when I was dating someone who Tom did not approve of he would refer to her as the devil. I would laugh…oh, how I laughed. Sadly when Monica or Kevin said the same thing I would cry. Weird eh? Tom could say anything to me.

The world of Summer Stage got an upgrade the following summer when Monica joined us. Monica and I had become friends in high school, and I was very happy she was going to be a Summer Stager.

Monica met Tom and Kevin and the four of us eventually became very close. To this day these three people are the friends that know me best and they surprisingly still like me.

After Summer Stage had ended that year, we decided to start an Improv group that would meet weekly. There were about ten of us, and we would go from house to house each week and play improv games for a couple of hours on Sunday nights. This was the kind of badass teen rebels we were.

So once every four or five weeks we would end up at my house, and that's when the shit storm would begin. Tom, Kevin and the other boys in the group would practice their ballet moves while we waited for everyone to show up, and that would be the fodder for my brother's mockery for weeks. For young teen boys in the late 70s, nothing was more mockable than boys who danced. My brothers had names for my friends, names like "fags," "dancers," "fag-dancers." Not a lot of variety, but my brothers made up for it with their relentlessness.

I knew that these three people would be in my life forever, and probably end up being closer to me than my brothers. Of course, they have, and they are and I am more grateful than I can ever say to a man named Harry Dietzler who started Summer Stage so some kids could put on some plays.

We did do lots of plays, but more than that we did a lot of finding out about ourselves and finding like-minded people and finding our futures. For me, I also found there a way to be true to myself.

Thank you, Harry.

CHAPTER 12

NUNS

There is an old saying in my family, "You can't go to Catholic school for twelve years and not run into some nuns." Actually, that is not an old saying; I just made it up. But it is true. The first nun to make an impression on me had such a beautiful face that I have never forgotten it. I was in first grade, and I had spilled my little box of pink alphabet letters in the hallway. I was so scared that I was going to get yelled at for dropping them and was hurrying to pick them all up when this sweet woman knelt down next to me and said, "Would you like some help?"

"Yes please, Sister." I just stared at her as she put all my letters into the box, I couldn't look at anything but her face, it was like porcelain…but natural. She looked at me staring at her, "Well your letters are all back where they belong, now where do you belong?" I wasn't sure if I should tell her what I was thinking, but I did anyway, "Sister, are you, Mary?" She smiled at me and said, "Do you mean the Virgin Mother?" I nodded. "No dear, I want to be like her, but I am not her." I guess I thought maybe she was Mary because everything I knew about "Mary" seemed to describe this woman. She was kind, beautiful and poised. I was mistaken about who she was, but I know now, as I did then, that she was like the "Mary" in my mind: caring, maternal and full of grace.

Not all the nuns I knew were like the first I remember. Some were downright mean, some were funny, and some were wacky. The fact is, there were as many different kinds of nuns as there is any other group of people. It is of import, however, that these nuns were teachers and had authority over me.

When I was in fourth grade, there was a classmate whose Mother had died. The girl returned to school one day after her Mother's funeral and just burst into tears. This nun sent her to the nurse's office. After she left the nun said that we should all take note, that if our mothers ever died and we "carried on" and cried like that, it would just mean that we had not helped our mother with the dishes. Although the statement made no sense and I was appalled that she had said it, I know I rushed home and did all the dishes that night, while hoping my mother realized how much I loved her. I did not believe what the nun had said, but it bothered me.

In sixth grade when we were mature enough to handle the facts, a nun told us about heaven. Your basic heaven rules were these: you get whatever you want in heaven if you have been good in this life. I had a restless mind and apparently a bit of an annoying one as well for this description of heaven caused me some logical challenges. I raised my hand and when called on asked, "Sister, let's say I die, and I have been good and all I want to do is be with my Mom, and my Mom dies and she has been good and all she wants to do is be with HER Mom. If we have both been good how can we both get what we want?"

My question upset the nun who seemed flustered and angry. "Miss Baker, you miss the point, for, in heaven, it's not like here. You probably wouldn't even recognize your Mother because in heaven we will all be white blobs of soul floating around."

This answer caused me terror. White blobs of soul? I didn't want to be a blob of soul! I could think of nothing else all day, and when I finally got home, I broke down crying and explained everything to my Dad, who as always had the wisest of answers to soothe my soul. "Ah Jane, you can't believe everything the nuns say, for Christ's sake they can't even balance a checkbook, that's why they became nuns in the first place." I didn't really know what a checkbook was nor did I care; I just wanted to know that I would recognize my Mom and Dad in heaven and not have to go up to every single white blob of soul and ask their name. My Father assured me that I would know him, and my Mom and all would be fine, so I stopped crying. I was, however, left with questions about why my father entrusted these checkbook-challenged women with my spiritual and intellectual growth.

Other nuns in my school life made idle, if not weird, threats that they never followed up on. One nun when I was in seventh grade was upset that I had made some remark that made my classmates chuckle. She was very soft-spoken, normally, but on this occasion she yelled in the loudest voice I had ever heard her use.

"Were you being FUNNY Miss Baker? Were you? Well, I'll show you funny!" She never did. Ever. Not one funny thing ever came out of her mouth. I waited all year to be shown funny; I was let down.

When I got into high school, I encountered nuns that I admired for their intelligence, kindness, and humor. The nun who was both a typing teacher and a guidance counselor was not one of them. When I was a freshman, I was failing three subjects. I didn't study, and my mind was much too worried on the inside for me to focus on much of anything. This typing teacher/counselor called me down to her office one day and inquired as to why I was failing three subjects. At this time in my life, I disguised my worries and troubles in humor. So I said, "Three? I thought I was only failing two!" The nun, whom I will call Sister Typewriter, for I forget her name, kept at me and asked me why I was not doing better. I didn't have an answer for her, so she sent me back to class.

I was sent to get an IQ test the next week. Again I was called to Sister Typewriter's office where I was told that the IQ test proved I was not unable to do the work, contrary to what she had assumed. She continued to pry into my life and ask questions as to why I was not doing the work. Finally, I told her that my brother David was very ill and was no longer going to school. When I returned home from school each day he wanted to play cards, and I could not say no to him. I began to cry and the nun asked me what I was crying about, was I worried that he was going to die? Just hearing someone say those words threw me and I really bawled. She seemed shocked and annoyed at the same time and sent me back to class. My parents told me when I got home that they had a meeting with Sister Typewriter the next day and wanted to know if I knew what it was about. I was terrified that they would find out that I had told Sister Typewriter my fears about David, and then I didn't know what would happen. The next day I was called down to Sister Typewriter's again, but, this time, my parents were seated in the office.

Sister Typewriter opened the conversation in a friendly way, "Mr. and Mrs. Baker, it seems that Mary Jane has a bit of a problem telling the truth." Both of my parents looked at me with heads tilted in confusion. Sister Typewriter was calling me a liar, and I was afraid she was calling me a family secret teller; I wasn't sure which was worse. My father asked what she meant, and Sister Typewriter said that I was making things up, one example was the lie that I had a brother so sick he could no longer attend school and that I feared he would die. Hearing this, my Mother broke into tears, and my Dad told me to go back to class. I left that room but stayed outside long enough to hear my father lay into Sister Typewriter with words that surely shocked her as he expressed his outrage and anger at having to display our family's heartache so openly. Oddly enough I passed all my classes that year, I continued to play cards every day with David, and I learned a great deal that year, not much of it in school, but a great deal about life.

There was a nun that played piano for the school shows; she played very badly, so badly that it sounded like she hit several keys to the right and left of the intended note. This led to us calling her Sister Mary Mittens.

Another nun taught Biology and would stumble into rants about our health that have scarred me for life. Once she asked us if we brushed our teeth. Thus begun the dental health rant that ended as all her cautionary tales did, with some girl she had taught dying a horrible death due to not heeding her advice. This girl, if she really existed, did not heed the advice of Sister Cataclysm and ended up with a root canal, the root canal got infected, the infected tooth had to be pulled, and when it was, the blood gushed out, and she died of blood loss. All because she didn't brush. There were similar stories that had to do with death from poor feminine hygiene (privates fell off), death due to ignoring safety precautions when hiking (tick-related deaths).

There was a feeling that it had been really bad luck to have gotten her as a teacher, for it seemed almost everyone she ever taught died a horrid avoidable death.

Once, when walking down the "up stairs"—which was something that you could actually do in my high school and something that only the brave dared do—I was stopped by a nun I only knew slightly. She asked me if I had any brothers and, of course, I said yes. She asked me if they ever threw a punch at me, again, of course, yes. Then, completely unsolicited, she offered me advice on how to punch someone in the face and not hurt my hand. Then she trotted on up the up staircase towards the chapel she was in charge of. Strange woman. Good advice, though.

One nun that made putting up with all the strange ones worth it was Sister Miriam; she let me call her "Mirs" if nobody else was around. She often told me that I would make a good nun. I always laughed. She was a confidant; I could tell her all about my family and the stuff happening there. It was not until I met her in junior year that I was at all open with an adult about my family. She had the best laugh of anyone. She was one woman I knew in my heart had become a nun because she was pulled by some force greater than all the other forces that pull. She was the purest person I have ever known. Pure. Honest. Joyful. She made me seriously contemplate becoming a nun, if only for a moment.

To this day, if I see a nun, and it is rare that I do, I have an odd mix of feelings. They are at once familiar and unknowable, intimate and distant. I think nuns today are probably apt to be in control of their own checking. I hope they are still looking like "Mary" to lost little girls.

CHAPTER 13

Monica My Monica

Monica and I met when we were sophomores in high school. Our school did a "Freshman Day" play each year to welcome the new freshman; Monica and I met trying out for the play. I can honestly not remember what the play was; it was always a spoof of a Broadway show. In later years, we did Annie and The Sound of Music. This show had a Huey, Dewey and Louie in it and I was cast as one of those, perhaps Huey?

I had one line; it might have actually been one word. Monica had gotten the much-coveted part of the vending machine; she had three or four lines, probably related to the price of her wares. One of the things Monica remembers about that time was that I decided that I needed the script, and she could copy her lines. I think we were to share it, but I was oddly possessive about the script that held the word I would say on stage. Monica and I became very close very fast; she often didn't know when I was kidding because I was a tad sarcastic.

The first year I knew her I went to her house for her birthday party, and my gift to her was one of those cheesy mini posters on a plaque that had a picture of a snotty-looking dog. It said something like "I am annoyed by people who don't know my greatness." The gist was that she was superior and cool. Monica was not sure if I was actually thinking that was funny or was mocking her. It was a while, maybe years before she told me that she didn't know how to take that gift.

The Catholic girls school we went to had daily mass that you could go to after lunch if you were free. These masses were often offered up for a particular cause or person's soul. Early in that first year of our friendship, the school had asked my parents if they could celebrate a mass for my brother David who had passed away the summer before. Monica and I were close and talked almost daily on the phone after school and at night. We talked about many things, our love of Carol Burnett, our forthcoming stardom and how we would spend our millions, our love of boys who were actually gay.

During school announcements one morning, they mentioned that the mass after lunch would be offered for David Baker, brother of Mary Jane Baker. Shortly after that, Monica and I passed in the hall.

Monica stopped me, "Jane, isn't that weird, there is another Mary Jane Baker at this school?"

"What do you mean Monica?"

"Didn't you hear that announcement? There is a mass for a David Baker, and his sister 'Mary Jane' goes here?"

Embarrassed, I said. "Actually, that is me, it's for my brother David, he died this summer."

"You don't have a brother that died!" Monica said, looking at me like she had no idea what game I was playing.

"Yeah, I do," I said.

Monica looked shocked and hurt. What kind of friendship did we have, if I had not told her something so important and huge?

I didn't know how to explain to her that my family was strange.

My mother often said to me, "Don't tell people your problems, they won't be your friends if you do." I took that to mean not to talk about David and what had happened. We didn't talk much about it in the house and when we did, if you cried, one parent would tell you to go to your room and not let the other parent see you crying because it would upset them. I know that my parents did the best they could, but sometimes I wonder what they thought? Didn't they know that we were just kids and that we were in pain? There was an unspoken, or maybe spoken, rule that getting upset about David might upset Patrick because he had the same illness. It often occurred to me that Pat might have thought us heartless, or thought we didn't miss David. I have come to believe that Pat was far more intuitive than I could have known at fifteen. I think he knew and appreciated every kindness, even misguided ones, shown to him. I was a good Irish Catholic and a good Baker, and kept the private things private, even, or especially, when it hurt.

Monica forgave me that screw-up and I think that it allowed me to experience real honesty with someone about me and my life for the first time. Monica and I went through so much together through the years. We were in many productions together. Godspell was an especially fun show we did together.

We went to college together, two of them. We both spent a year at Penn State's local campus and then went to Hofstra University together. I don't know what Monica's main reason for choosing Hofstra was, but mine was that she would be there. While at Penn State, we would often car pool. One day we did not and while driving home we were in our cars driving side by side when we both heard over the radio that the pope had been shot. We looked at each other, and although the pope being shot was both weird and sad, we ended up laughing hysterically for we were in separate cars on a highway and with one simple look we were both able to relay our thoughts, which consisted of, "who shoots the pope?"

When carpooling, we often toyed with the emotions of the people waiting for their busses. We would roll down the windows and make the most absurd faces while yelling "MORNING!"

Not exactly deviant behavior, but for Catholic schoolgirls we considered ourselves fairly scandalous.

(Here is a photo of us reenacting this bizarre behavior.)

That's Monica on the left and me on the right.

When we went to Hofstra, a new world was ours. One particularly pivotal conversation occurred on the 13th floor of Tower F where the laundry facilities were. I had been thinking about my sexuality and had yet to talk to Monica about it. We started talking about all our friends and which ones were gay and which were not.

Out of nowhere I remember saying, "Monica, I can't be gay."

"Oh? Why not Jane?" she asked in a really loving mother like way.

"Well, when you go to sleep with a man, he puts his arm around you and protects you from the world right? And a woman can't do that?"

Monica thought for a second and then spoke, "Jane, no man can do that, nobody can do that," she told me.

I just stared at her until she asked me, "Is that your only reason Jane?"

"Yeah. That's all I got," I said.

"Oh Janey, you are gay hun." Monica came over and hugged me.

"Do you really think so Mon?" I thought maybe she was not sure.

"Absolutely," she replied.

"Wow, when did start thinking this?" I asked.

"Hmmm, well remember when we first met?" she asked.

"Yeah, freshman day auditions," I answered.

"Then. I first thought it then," she told me.

"What? Really? You are kidding me right?" I asked her.

How could Monica have known something I was just figuring out?

"Oh Jane, you're the gayest girl I know," and with this statement I began to accept it myself.

This conversation helped me a lot. Monica and I have shared so much, but not in that "Children's Hour" kind of way. I love Monica as much today as I did that night when she helped me figure myself out. Nothing can erase the experiences we shared. No time or distance can ever be so much that a mere phone call or email can't immediately bring her next to me.

Once, when she was intoxicated I assume, Monica said she wished I were a boy, so she could marry me. It's the only time in my life I wished I was a boy.

High School Reunion

2015 Outfest

CHAPTER 14

A Bit of 1985

I moved to NYC with my friends after graduating from college. I don't mean we all got apartments in various parts of NYC, I mean we all moved into the same apartment. There were five of us: Monica, Tom, Kevin, Penny and me. The apartment was on 46th Street. It was a sublet; I don't recall who secured it for us. It was a studio meant for one Dobby but instead housed five Hagrids.

We all slept on a pullout couch that was so beat up and small that it became a goal to get to bed first, so you didn't end up sleeping in the worst spot, called "the crevasse." This couch was cheap; it was a foam sofa that converted into a flatter surface, but by no means would you call this a bed. The crevasse existed where the former back and arms of the sofa unfolded to create the "bed." If you were unlucky enough to sleep in the crevasse you would most likely awaken from a dream where you were in a coffin, then you would realize it was not a dream, that you were stuck. The avoidance behavior around the crevasse became so unhealthy that people were feigning illnesses so they could argue it was for that reason they were going to bed at five o'clock; it had nothing to do with the crevasse.

The only entertainment we could afford was the free cable channel we were able to see on the TV. It was a public access channel. During the day, we all went out looking for jobs. At night, we watched the news on our channel. This news show was different then what I grew up watching, in that the news I watched as a child had newscasters who wore clothes. This newscast was done naked. They were not covering porn news or nudist colony news, just the news, naked. There was a rumor that our channel got more risqué after ten o'clock, but because of the crevasse, none of us could verify this.

Luckily we did not stay in this apartment for long. We found another apartment that was huge, by comparison, right around the corner at 46th and 10th. We signed that lease, and we moved there as quickly as they would let us and kissed the naked news goodbye. We built a few structures in the new apartment that made it feel like there were rooms. There was a loft bed that Tommy and I shared, and under it was our closet space. There was a pullout couch that Monica and Penny shared. There was only one single bed, and since Kevin bought it, he got to sleep in it. We built a divider/closet that separated the main room from the kitchen and bathroom, and Monica and Penny kept all their things stored in there. Soon, a company called Ticket Call employed us all. If you wanted theater tickets, you would call, and we would happily charge them to your credit card. I can't recall anyone that worked there that was not working or trying to work in the "business." Actually, everyone in New York was in the "business."

Once, a therapist told me she had to cancel our next appointment because she had an audition for a film and offered to show me her SAG card. It crossed my mind that she was just portraying a therapist in some elaborate method acting exercise. I stopped seeing her.

CHAPTER 15

Dracula, Starring Tina Fey

The summer after Patrick died I began teaching again at Upper Darby Summer Stage. I had taught there on and off for years, and it was a great way for me to get back into life.
It was at the beginning of that summer that I became friends with Tina Fey. An incredibly accurate account of that friendship is in Tina's book Bossypants. People often ask me if I knew when I met Tina that she would be hugely famous. Of course not. People also ask me if I was shocked when she because hugely famous. Of course not. I knew immediately that she was a peer and a friend, despite the fact that she was seventeen, and I was twenty-four. That she eventually married a guy ten years older than her proves either that she has always been mature for her age or that all the older people around her are infantile. I'm happy for her either way.

One thing I always think of when I think of the house she lived in and her very intelligent, funny family is that her brother, Peter, had the most incredibly diverse collection of CDs. It was from these CDs that Tina made me a present for a birthday or something of an assortment of female singers. She labeled the tape "Whim Moan." Once, Tina and I sat in a Pizza Hut one night thinking up slogans for T-shirts. One of them was a spoof of all the different spellings of women that were floating around in those days.

The idea was to have several options, like womyn or womon, crossed out and the remaining option being Whim Moan. I think that this is where Pizza Hut came up with its slogan "The Pizza Place for Parody."
I first heard Roseanne Cash, early Linda Ronstadt, and a very young k.d. lang on that tape. I'd like to thank Tina publicly for introducing me to k.d. lang's music. I'd also like to (publicly) ask Tina to introduce me to k.d. lang.

I belly laughed with Tina more times than I can remember, either during improv or just hanging around. One experience that we shared remains one of my fondest memories of live theater ever.

After the summer, I was hired by Upper Darby High School to teach its drama club and to direct its fall show.

I decided to stage Dracula, and to make a Halloween event out of it, hosting a haunted house during the day of the Saturday performance. The result was the most epic theatrical weekend ever.

I held auditions early in September, and there were several kids who stood out. There was a heavy metal-looking guy who could easily play Dracula and look awesome doing it. His brother was a funny character type and an obvious choice for the role of the doctor who runs the asylum. There was a fella named Nick who was a talented actor and could play weird, so Renfield he was. Lucy was easy, as a beautiful young waif auditioned and the character was a beautiful young waif. For her love interest, I think the character's name was John Harker; a young man gave the single best audition for anything I had ever directed. (This will be important later, so if you have a highlighter, mark that last sentence.)

The play had six major parts for guys, and I had five guys who were good. The problem with high school theater, or theater, or film or even the world actually, is that there are so few good parts for the girls. I had yet to cast Van Helsing, the lead, if you don't count the vampire. This part was huge and had to be played by someone who could do that thing called "acting." I didn't have a guy up to it. I did have a Fey. So we switched the gender of the role, and Tina played Professor Van Helsing. If a role didn't have a love interest or some other plot element that made it imperative that it be played by the gender it was written for, I might change it to give girls more roles. In this case, it was a great idea. I was able to cast a very talented person who otherwise would not have been cast with a simple gender reassignment by pen.

Rehearsals went well, and by opening weekend we had a (sorta) strong show, a great-looking set, and an excited cast and crew. Opening night went without a hitch; people screamed, wet their pants, and cheered when Van Helsing spiked Heavy Metal Dracula to death.

The following day was our haunted house. We already had the very scary set on the stage, and all the kids involved with the production were bringing in their own stuff to set up a "fright station." Our actors were to take the crowds from station to station. Some stations were filled with creepy stuffed bodies without heads, or bowls of raw eggs that people put their hands into and were told were eyeballs. Lots of gross stuff, but completely in the norm of haunted house fare. Before opening the haunted house, Tina and I went around to the stations and approved of them and declared them ready or in need of improvement. At one station a very sweet, obviously somewhat disturbed little boy from the tech crew sat outside a structure made of bamboo.

"So what's the theme here, fella?" I asked.

He turned around, revealing camouflage paint on his face and an army jacket on his body. As he spoke, Tina and I looked into the bamboo cage. "It's a prisoner-of-war hut, without food or water, and the guy in there is dying."

"Wow," Tina and I both said.

We huddled up a few feet away from the little guy.

"That's fucked up, right?" I asked.

"Yeah, really messed up," Tina said.

"Okay, we need to not let this happen, right?" I asked.

"I would shut it down, Jane," Tina said. So we did. We told him that it was just too scary and that instead he should make it into a random scary thing. He removed all signs of Cambodia and the military except for his camo paint, which he said he could not get off.

We opened the haunted house, and it was really cool. The lights were low and focused on the coffin on the set. There was spooky music and a line around the auditorium waiting to get in. Things were going swell. Then the power went out for a second and came right back on with the house lights up full and the music stopped. Now the theater didn't look scary; it looked stupid. Nobody was scared anymore; they were laughing. The tech crew quickly reset the lights and got the mood back, but the audio wasn't working. Tina and I were watching everything from the booth, and the sound tech handed me a microphone so I could say scary things over the sound system. I had nothing. I could not think of one scary thing to say. Tina looked puzzled. A quiet Jane was rare. Then it occurred to me. "Tina, what is your real name again?" I knew that she had told me once and that it sounded scary to me. Although it is spelled Vasiliki Stamatina Fey, to me, it sounded like this: "Bastalikeeee Stam a teena," which is what I wailed over the sound system. It was creepy. After a while Tina said, "Yo, you're scaring people with my name!"

"I know, isn't that awesome?"

Tina didn't think it was awesome, and she unplugged my mic. Quick and clear, Fey shut me down. The music came back on, so it wasn't so terrible, but the music was only a fraction of how scary Tina's name sounded.

After the successful haunted house, we turned around and got ready for the show. That night the show was a nonstop suck fest. I was watching from the audience and was torn between crying and laughing hysterically. I might have done both at one time or another during the debacle.

Here is a partial list of what went wrong.

At the introduction of Dracula for the first time there was a dramatic spotlight on the doors that he entered from. He would come in with the spotlight on him, flare out his Dracula cape, and the chamber he had come from having been previously filled with fog from a fog machine, be surrounded by fog, to great melodramatic effect. Except the fog machine started late and when the doors opened it looked like a tiny poof came out of Dracula's butt.

The spotlight was supposed to stay on him for a few seconds but went off very quickly, and a light came up just as quickly on another actor onstage completely spacing out and not ready for light; he looked directly into the light and grimaced. So that was the second laugh of the night.

The fog machine was turned off but sputtered throughout the first act, randomly farting fog.

The actor, who had auditioned excellently, had the line "Professor, what is a vampire?" This was the cue for Tina to launch into a three-page monologue on vampires, vampire history, how to kill a vampire, all things vampire. She made it interesting, and it was a pleasure to see the audience riveted by her delivery. The speech ended with "And that, young man, is a vampire." The actor Tina was directing this information to was to say, "Oh, this is horrible." Instead, he repeated, "Professor, what is a vampire?" I almost died trying not to laugh. Tina had a look of total exasperation on her face, and I didn't know how she would get out of this, but thank God for her quick thinking and mad improv skills. "You are clearly exhausted son," she said. "Go to bed." The audience never knew there had been a mistake, and the other actor, although he had more lines, did as he was told and exited the stage.

Later in the act a bat would fly across the stage and disappear into the darkness. Now, when one plans to have a bat come down out of the corner of the rigging and fly across the stage, one directs the cast to react with screams and shock and pointing and such, then when the bat is gone to act relieved but still upset. Instead of cruising across the stage, the bat got stuck in the middle of the wire almost center stage. One of the most bizarre things I've ever seen is a cast of kids reacting in shock to a diving bat and then having no relief because it just stays. I would have assumed that were you to script what the actors looked like they were thinking, in character, it might have been, "Hmmm, I'm horrified by that bat, but it's not leaving, so I will keep a cautious eye on it and proceed with my life." Now and then an actor would look up at the bat, almost lovingly, as if it were a pet bird. That was the first act.

At one point in the second act Dracula is in a room with Van Helsing and when he looks into a mirror, the mirror is supposed to shatter. Dracula would look at the mirror, it would shatter, and Tina as Van Helsing would say something like "Aha! You're a vampire." Well, the mirror didn't shatter, but the actor playing Dracula acted as if it did, baring his fangs and looking exceedingly strange!

Tina said something smart and quick like, "Your reflection, it's not in the mirror! Aha! You're a vampire." The scene continued, but backstage the young tech-crew fella who had set up the Cambodian prisoner-of-war scenario for our haunted house was most unhappy that his rigging had failed. He set out to make things right, crawling under the stage until he could go no further, then crawling out from under the side of the stage, in clear view of the audience. Well, not totally clear, because he still had his camo paint on, but you could definitely tell there was a small boy crawling around with something in his hand.

Camo boy in clear view of audience.

hammer

He arrived at the other side of the mirror, slowly raised the hammer up toward the mirror, and cocked his hand. Remember, the cast had moved on, still in the room with the mirror but way too far away from the event for a mirror shatter to make any sense. THUMP. Small boy hit mirror. It did not shatter but made the cast turn around to see what had made that noise. They returned to the scene and the small camo boy hit it again. Thump. Again, no breaking. Finally the third hit shattered the mirror, but this time the cast didn't even look. The boy crawled back, mission accomplished.

Toward the end of the play, as Van Helsing and the others were following Dracula to his coffin, they went down an awesome stairway painted so wonderfully to look like stone, but it wasn't stone, it was foam. Highly flammable foam. Getting too close to the foam, one of the candle-carrying cast members set the wall on fire. The foam burned fast, but fortunately the fire was contained to the two or three feet of foam the actor lit with the candle.

You would think that once you set fire to a piece of a set, you would stop putting the flame on it, but that was not the instinct of said actor. It almost looked like he thought he could put the fire out with more fire. In an effort to help, the very talented Renfield tried to get to the fire, but because he was blind without his glasses and the asshole director wouldn't let him use them, he tumbled from near the balcony stairs, found himself right in front of the coffin that the cast was traveling toward, and ran away, through the fog-fart doors. A poof of fog marked his exit.

My little buddy in the camo paint walked right onto the stage with a fire extinguisher and put the fire out but not before Tina's father stood up and yelled "Fire!" Tina's dad, or Mr. Fey as I call him, was a man of action; the fire was out by the time he sat down, thank God.

Path camo boy took to put out fire!

Closing night people screamed, but for different reasons than the opening night. Rather than cheering when Tina/Van Helsing spiked Heavy Metal Dracula to death, people were giggling. Not the expected reaction, but considering that a toddler had walked out onto the stage and looked right into the coffin as Tina tried to kill Dracula, it did seem fitting. Finally the play ended, and I feel fairly accurate in saying that this might have been the scariest Dracula performance ever.

PART THREE

Gay Nesssss

H i I'm
gay. So are you. M aybe. Maybe not. I
don't care. Just don't egg my house. Ok? Hi
I'm gay. So are you. Maybe. Maybe not. I don't car
e. Just don't egg my house. Ok? Hi I'm gay. So are yo
u. Maybe. Maybe not. I don't care. Just don't egg my
house. Ok? Hi I'm gay. So are you. Maybe. Maybe not. I
don't care. Just don't egg my house. Ok? Hi I'm gay. S
o are you. Maybe. Maybe not. I don't care. Just don't
egg my house. Ok? Hi I'm gay. So are you. Maybe
. Maybe not. I do n't care. Just d
on't egg my hous
e. Ok? H i I'm gay
. So are you. Maybe. Maybe not. I don't care. Just don't egg
my house. Ok? Hi I'm gay. So are you. Maybe. Maybe not. I d
on't care. Just don't eg
g my ho use. Ok?
Hi I'm ga y. So are
you. May be. Mayb
e not. I d on't care
. Just don 't egg m

CHAPTER 16

Gay Trade

A few days before Christmas 1985 I was on the train from NYC to Philly. There was a terrible snowstorm, and I was getting concerned that I might end up stuck at the 30th street station. My Dad was to pick me up but all the other passengers were talking about how terrible the storm was and I was beginning to think maybe Dad might not make it. I should not have worried since nobody loved to prove he could drive in a storm more than Joe Baker. It always struck me as odd that my Dad would go out in any storm and then announce, "OK, here we go! Let's see what loons came out in this?" I always wanted to have a mirror handy when he said that but never did. When I got off the train and went out to our meeting place, I was happy to see my Dad triple parked reading a pocket novel. "Who's winning the war?" I asked my Dad as I got in the car. "We are, we always do! Hi honey, it's great to have you home," he said as he kissed my cheek. My Dad loved reading novels about the war. I never quite understood the fascination, as the outcome seemed pretty predictable. It made me very happy when he moved on to mystery novels that took place during the war. The snow was pretty intense, and it was hard to see very far in front of us. The traffic was slowing down considerably, and I began to feel awkward with the silence in the car, I realize now I should have been fonder of the silence. My father had known about my being gay for a little over a year, and he had not taken it very well. By this time, Pat's health and happiness were much more consuming and critical to my parents than my being gay, or so I had thought.

"So Jane, I've been thinking," my Dad said.

Terror filled my soul.

My father never thought.

This could only be bad.

"Yeah?" I said, "How did that go?"

"Don't be a smart ass, you're not that smart… you ass." He always chuckled when he said this. He thinks he made it up, maybe he did. I laughed too because frankly, if we were laughing we were not talking about the thing he had thought about and I was all for that!

"So…. as I was saying, I've been thinking. I know that you think you are gay…but I have a few questions."

"THINK?" If you can't sleep for a couple of nights, you might think you have insomnia. I don't think I ever thought I was gay. Do people think they might be right-handed? Do people think they might be Irish? I was gay because I fell in love with women. I didn't believe I needed to think about it at all.

I decided to be patient and kind because that's just the kind of gay girl I thought I was.

"OK Dad, what do you want to ask me?"

He paused for a few seconds.

"Jeez Jane, as a father you don't ever imagine having a conversation like this with your daughter. I guess…I just want to know that you are sure of it."

There are times in your life when you want a wild animal to swoop in and pull your head off and fly away with it leaving those behind to deal with your abandoned body. This was one of those times.

"I'm quite sure of it Dad," I said.

Dad was now on a roll. "Well Jane, you say that, but, jeez, this is hard to ask… but have you ever slept with a man?"

I was now thinking of ways to self-induce a massive heart attack or stroke. I had nothing!

"Wow Dad, um, no...no I have not." I didn't know what to say except the truth; it seemed only fair since he was obviously killing a bit of himself to have this conversation in the first place.

My Dad continued, "Well see, I was thinking, Beauregard, (not his real name) is a nice boy, don't you think?"

Beauregard was my brother Pat's best friend much like a brother to me.

"Beauregard is the nicest guy in the world Dad. There is nobody better," I said.

"Yeah, see...I thought that maybe you and Beauregard...oh jeez." I felt bad for my father, but I couldn't think of anything to say. "So, I thought...as a favor to me...you might...you love me right Jane?"

"Yes Dad, of course, I love you." I said as his plan was becoming clear.

My Dad looked so anxious I couldn't stand to watch him struggling.

"Dad, if you are asking me to sleep with Beauregard to prove to you that I am a lesbian, I will do that because I love you that much."

The relief on his face was unmistakable.

"You love me, right Dad?" I asked him.

"Of course I do Jane." he assured me.

"Well then we have a deal, I'll sleep with a guy if you will," I said.

"What?" The relief left his face faster than it had appeared.

"You have never slept with a guy, right? So how do you know you are straight if you don't try it? I'm just saying that I will if you will."

A couple of seconds passed and he looked at me as if he had figured out one of the great mysteries of life.

"Ohhhhhhh...wait...are you saying that the thought of YOU having sex with a man makes YOU feel the same way that the thought of ME having sex with a man makes ME feel?"

"Pretty much Dad," I said as I watched it all sink in.

"Ok, we don't ever have to talk about it again."

We spent the rest of the ride home listening to Christmas carols on the radio, and my Dad only spoke again right before I got out of the car. "I love you, Jane." I went around to his side of the car and opened his door, kissed him on the cheek and said, "I love you too."

That year I spent Christmas at home with a Dad that sorta understood me and a brother I thought might not have another Christmas. When I returned to NYC, I found out I had lost my job. Fair enough.

CHAPTER 17

No Longer Not Gay

1982

Hello.

Hi.

Are you following me?

Yes.

Why?

Because. You are Mary Jane Baker.

Why do you care?

Because I like your eyes.

Really, what color are they?

Blue, very blue.

Aren't we in a class together?

I sit behind you in Seigman's class.

Right behind me?

I couldn't see you if I sat right behind you.

Would that matter?

Yes.

Why?

It just would.

Copying my notes?

Hardly.

Why not?

You take lousy notes.

I do?

You draw.

I draw?

Doodle.

I doodle do I?

You do doodle.

I suppose I do.

You do!

And?

And what?

Why are you at this party?

Am I not allowed to be here?

It's not my party.

I know.

So you know Joey?

Very close friend. He told me.

Told you what?

What I wanted to know.

What did he say?

He said "Mary Jane Baker."

I see.

Do you?

I think I do.

Tell me.

I see that he told you my name?

So what was the question?

I assume it was, "what is 'her' name?"

No.

Then I don't know.

Well if you want to know I'll tell you.

Ok.

Ok, you want to know?

No! "Ok," that you'll tell me if I want to know.

I asked him another question.

I don't want to know.

How about if I tell you just the answer?

Not sure I want to hear it.

The answer was "I think she'd kiss you back."

Oh Jesus.

Figure out the question?

Yes, I'm not completely stupid!

I never said you were.

Hmmm.

So…was he right?

What?

Would you kiss back?

Kiss who back?

Me.

You?

Yes.

No.

Why not?

HMMM …well, let's see, you're a girl….

And?

So am I…

And?

You're a lesbian…

True.

I am not.

False.

How would you know?

I just know.

Oh, are you psychic?

No.

So you don't know. I'm NOT gay.

Ok.

Really.

Ok.

I'm not!

I believe you.

No you don't.

Yes I do.

Where did everyone go?

I don't know.

What album is this?

Face Value…Phil Collins.

I like it.

Me too.

Hmmm.

Wanna dance?

No.

Fast or slow.

No.

Can I kiss you?

No.

Why not?

Because I said so.

Ok.

Ok.

Ok?

No.

Ok!

We should go.

We should stay.

Why?

Why not?

I'm not gay.

I know that.

Good.

I was thinking…

What?

If you're not gay…

Which I am not…

Then kissing me wouldn't kill you.

No.

Then you'd know for sure.

I already know.

Absolutely?

Positively!

So one kiss couldn't change that.

Not likely to.

Ok…

I better go.

Why?

Because I'm afraid.

Of what?

Of you.

Why?

You know why.

Are you afraid of me, or of yourself?

I don't know.

Do you want to find out?

I don't know.

May I kiss you?

I don't know.

Will you punch me if I try?

I might.

I might.

Might what?

Might try.

Ok.

Ok?

You might try.

Ok, here is what I am going to do…this song is almost over…

Ok.

If you are still standing here, looking at me the way you are now when the next song starts…I am going to kiss you.

Hmmm.

Ok?

I understand.

Still afraid?

Yes.

Why?

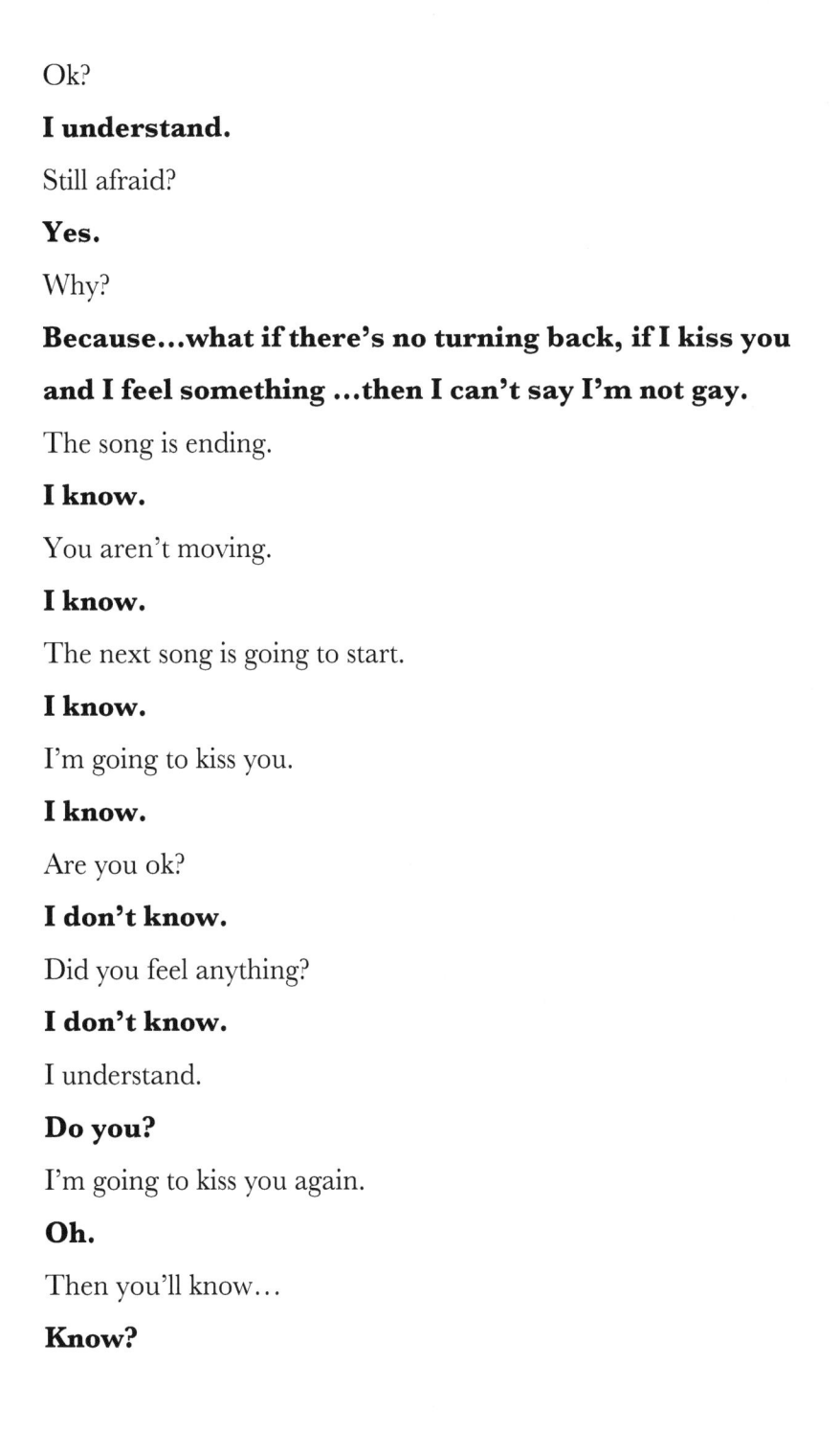

Because…what if there's no turning back, if I kiss you and I feel something …then I can't say I'm not gay.

The song is ending.

I know.

You aren't moving.

I know.

The next song is going to start.

I know.

I'm going to kiss you.

I know.

Are you ok?

I don't know.

Did you feel anything?

I don't know.

I understand.

Do you?

I'm going to kiss you again.

Oh.

Then you'll know…

Know?

If you feel anything.

Ok.

Mary Jane Baker!

Yes?

Wow.

What?

You are kissing me back!

I know.

Ok.

Do you want me to stop?

No.

No?

No!

Ok.

But l have a question.

Yes.

Yes what?

The answer is yes…I felt something.

And…are you ok?

Yeah…I think so.

CHAPTER 18

Let's Go On An Outing!

In 1982, I was nineteen years old. I had recently started figuring out that I was a big gaybird. I had always felt different, but I had assumed that was because I grew up in the house I grew up in, in the family I grew up in. I also thought my "difference" was probably that I was a silly person. As described in an earlier essay, a panic attack was the result of my actual focusing on my sexuality for five minutes. I was fairly sure after the panic that the reason I was panicky was not because some girl was obviously flirting with me; the problem was I liked that she was flirting. I liked that she kissed me. I liked sex, with women. This last sentence is what has led me to the firm belief that I am a lesbian. Although I was coming to terms with the fact that I was gay, I was so distraught by the fact that I knew this would devastate my parents. You know how when something changes about you that you are sure that people can see it on your face? Well having recently gotten "de'lesbo" tattooed on my forehead I was sure my parents might suspect. Just kidding, no tattoo, not on my forehead anyway!

Sometime in the spring of 1982, I was deflowered—relinquished my maidenhead, became a woman, loving woman—whatever euphemism you like. From the moment I knew I was gay, I also felt great stress and fear that my parents would find out. We were not a family that spoke openly about anything, so a conversation about sex was hardly likely. Even though I knew my family was not about to ask anything about my personal life, I was a nervous wreck worrying about how they would react. I had the support of all my friends, most of whom were gay, and some of us came out to each other at the same time. During a rehearsal for a play we were both in, one of my very best friends rushed up to me with hickies all over him and said, "You put these hickies on my neck." "No, I didn't," I said. "Just say you did!" he begged. "Okay, but you have to tell me who put them there," I said. "Rob," he said. "You are gay! Guess what, I think I'm gay!" We laughed and hugged and laughed and then I felt sick because the whole cast thought I put hickies all over my friends neck. So gross.

I went to the college counseling seeking peace and someone to talk me down and center me. My parents were not fans of therapists, counselors, head shrinkers, social workers or witch doctors. My parents were fans of priests. Anyone who was known to have gone to any of these charlatans was deemed a "nut," "loopy," "off the deep end," "gone fishing," "cracker barrel," or just "crazy." If anyone was unfortunate enough to have a nervous breakdown, my mother would say, "I wish I had the luxury of a breakdown." I was always a bit confused by this statement. What part of any movie where they show someone having a breakdown looked luxurious? So clearly going to the counseling center was a big step for me. When you have grown up thinking your parents are wise and all-knowing, you will later have to face the fact that a.) You are gullible and b.) You have to get over a lot of shit to see a counselor.

I got over my shit and went to the registration desk and asked to see someone. The student worker asked me if I was "in crisis." I didn't know if I was in a crisis or not, I just wanted to talk to a counselor, so I said that. "Oh, well if it's not a crisis how about next month?" So I said, "It's a crisis, I'm gay." A few minutes later I was invited into a room and waited for my counselor. I was hoping for a hip, young, cool person that would be tapped into current research and changing tides about gay people. Instead, my grandmother walked in. At least, she looked like, dressed like, spoke like and acted like my grandmother. This was all fine because the reason I was there was her counseling acuity. I explained that I realized I was gay and that I loved my parents so much, and I didn't want to hurt them. She asked me what else had changed lately and what else was going on, had I lost weight? Had I lost weight?

"Um, actually, I've been so worried lately that I have lost weight, like around twenty pounds the last couple months."

Grandma stared at me, "And this same-sex event that took place, was that after the weight loss?"

As new to this gay thing as I was I knew "same-sex event" was a huge red flag. "I guess so, yeah," I said.

Then she opened my eyes to a whole new way of thinking about my sexuality. "Is it possible, just possible, that when you were very fat, nobody found you attractive, and when you lost weight, it just so happened that the first person you noticed paying you any attention was a woman, and that's why you think you are gay?"

I thought about this possibility for a moment. "No, that's absurd." She stared at me again, for a bit longer this time. "Well you seem like you've made up your mind," She said. I really didn't know what to make of her. "I didn't come here because I'm confused, I came because I am afraid that I will hurt my parents! Am I the first gay person you have had as a client?" I asked. "Well yes and no, some of my students might have been gay but I wouldn't have known that, I'm a career counselor." I left. I did feel better. I knew that if I didn't want to be gay anymore I just needed to get fat again.

As my friends and I headed home for the holidays, I felt very nervous, I just knew that my family would know. I just had a very terrible feeling about this trip home; I knew it was going to be bad. But not being a psychic I assumed I was just making a big deal out of nothing. I was very wrong, about being wrong.

Christmas night at around 11:45 I was sitting in my sister's room chatting about something when we heard my parents pull up to the house. "Are they drunk?" I asked my sister. "Can't tell yet. Shhh." We listened, and it was pretty clear they were both tanked. "Shit. I'm going to my room," I said as I bolted toward the stairs to the third floor. "I'm asleep," Joanne said as she turned off her light.

My parents came in the house loudly, and I was thinking how smart it was that Pat had Timmy put him to bed rather than wait for my dad to get home.

I was so on edge during that visit that I had not even unpacked. I'd been there for days and was living out of my duffle bag. As I lay on my bed, I listened to their footsteps and realized that they were coming straight up to bed. No squabble? This was unusual. My parents didn't fight all that often. Usually, it was my mom telling my dad he drank too much. Duh. The trifecta of irrational arguing, inane allegations, and befuddling slurs was most often reached when both parents were sufficiently trashed. This was such a night. The evening ending without an epic confrontation was statistically impossible. And statistics are real. So was the confrontation. From their movements I could tell that my dad had gone to the bathroom, gotten into bed and immediately fallen asleep as evidenced by the snore-a-thon he started.

My mother had not changed into her sleepwear yet and was clickity clacking across the floor of the hallway. She didn't make noise walking in her room as the freshly raked shag carpet muffled her steps. I heard her light a cigarette and began to relax if they were not arguing there would be no reason for her to call me to referee the fight.

"Mary Jane, come here," She said from her room. I froze; I wanted no part of this. I was not budging, not answering, not engaging in crazy this time.

"Mary Jane, I know you are awake, I saw Joanne turn her light off…." I stayed silent. If I could just get past this invitation to the nuthouse dance, I would be home free.

"Joanne, did Jane just go upstairs?" my mother asked my sister.

"Yep," my sister said. I don't blame her; she wanted to live.

"Jane, I know you just went upstairs, come here," she demanded.

"Why? I'm sleepy." I said. I hoped that whatever it was, she could ask Joanne instead.

"We are all sleepy damn it, get down here!" Something told me that Joanne would not do in this case.

I went downstairs and stood in the doorway of my parent's room. "Yes?" I said.

"I like those pajamas." I had not gotten changed, furthering the accumulation of facts that I had lied; I was not asleep, not even close.

"I fell asleep in my clothes. Is that what you wanted, to make sure I changed?" I asked jokingly.

"No," she said, as she exhaled her smoke into my general area, killing all hope I had of this not being a horrible night. "I want to talk to you."

"You are talking to me," I said.

"Don't be a smart-ass." She waited until she could see that I was sufficiently nervous and continued. "Your Uncle John has a very lonely life. You know that right?" It wasn't a question even though there is a question mark there. It was a declaration of what this discussion was about and her opinion of the topic. We all knew my father's brother John was gay.

"Um, I think Uncle John's loneliness might have more to do with his being an asshole," I said.

"Oh, do you think so? You don't think it's the way he chooses to live his life?"

And so the following scene began:

Me: I don't think Uncle John chose to be gay Mom.

Mom: What did he choose then?

Me: He chose to be an asshole.

Mom: He didn't choose to not be gay!

Me: I don't think it's a choice. I think it's just how you are born.

Mom: Oh, so it's the parent's fault?

Me: I didn't say that.

Mom: Oh, so whose fault is it?

Me: I don't think it's a fault.

Mom: Oh really?

Me: Yes, really.

Mom: I suppose your friends are gays.

Me: Some are.

Mom: Oh that's wonderful.

Me: What?

Mom: Some of your friends are gays, that's great!

Me: I don't know why it matters.

Mom: You wouldn't would you?

Me: Mom, Uncle John is lonely; some of my friends are gay. So what?

Mom: Is Monica a gay?

Me: No.

Mom: Of course not.

Me: What?

Mom: She wouldn't do that to her mother.

Me: What are you talking about? She's not gay because she's not gay.

Mom: What about Bill? What about Donny?

Me: Bill is. I don't know about Donny.

Mom: Bill is?

Me: Yes.

Mom: Well I hope he didn't tell his parents.

Me: Why?

Mom: Why? Why do you think? So he wouldn't ruin their lives!

Me: Oh, well I think he did tell them.

Mom: How selfish.

Me: He wasn't being selfish.

Mom: I think it's selfish.

Me: He was upset, he broke up with someone that he had been dating for a very long time, he was crying and was sad.

Mom: So he told them. What did he have to tell them?

Me: He told them because they asked him why he was crying.

Mom: He couldn't have lied?

Me: Lied? No, he doesn't lie to his parents.

Mom: Well it would have been kinder. What did they do?

Me: They told him they loved him.

Mom: Oh they did?

Me: Yeah, they wanted him to see a therapist but the therapist was really weird. So they don't want him to go anymore, and I guess they are just okay about it now...or becoming okay with it.

Mom: How was the therapist weird? Not thinking gay is normal? I must be weird too because it's not normal Jane!

Me: Well the therapist did think it was abnormal, and his idea was to put electric shocks on Bill's testicles and shock him when he showed him a picture of a man and not shock him when he saw a picture of a woman. Great idea right? That's so normal!

Mom: Watch your tone.

Me: Well that's pretty crazy right, electrocuting someone?

Mom: Of course that's awful. Of course, but there might have been another doctor they could send him to.

Me: Mom, there's nothing wrong with Bill.

Mom: Well we disagree. I assume his parents probably wish he never said a word about it.

Me: I don't think so.

Mom: Monica's not a gay.

Me: I know that.

Mom: Of course Monica is just normal. Selma must be relieved.

Me: What do you mean?

Mom: She didn't have to see her daughter come home in a man's coat.

Me: What?

Mom: That coat you wore home. It's a man's coat Jane! I'm not stupid.

Me: It's Monica's coat, well it's our coat, we bought it together, at a thrift store, it's just my week to wear it.

Mom: That's a lie.

Me: What is?

Mom: Monica wouldn't wear that coat.

Me: It's our coat mom.

Mom: I bet it is.

Me: It's a stupid coat, why would I lie about a coat?

Mom: I wish I knew. I wish I knew something.

Then my mom paused, for a long time. I had still not entered her room nor did I want to. I just wanted to get out. I was so confused by what she was saying, or not saying. Gay isn't normal. Don't tell your family. Why even talk about this? I realized that this was a warning, not to say anything about myself. I was fine with that idea.

> Mom: If one of my kids were a gay, I would never accept it. I wouldn't approve of them or their lifestyle, but I would still love them.

Now I was more tangled. She would still love them… but why? She wouldn't approve or accept them, what's to love? This felt like a trap, but you don't expect to get trapped by your parents. What did she want?

> Mom: If one of my kids were gay, I wouldn't accept it but I would love them.
>
> Me: That's good Mom.
>
> Mom: What a sad and lonely life.
>
> Me: Mom, things are changing, and you don't have to be lonely and sad…

She cut me off.

> Mom: What would you know? I know, it's lonely, it's sad.
>
> Me: That's your generation Mom, not mine.
>
> Mom: If one of my kids were gay, I would not accept it, but I would love them.
>
> Me: I heard you, mom.

Now she was poking my father with her non-smoking hand

Mom: Joe, wake up. Joe! Wake up! Joe!

Dad: What Delores?

Mom: Joe, what would you do if one of your kids told you they were gay?

Dad: What?

Mom: What would you do if one of your kids told you they were gay?

My dad didn't even turn over.

Dad: If one of my kids was queer, it would break my heart. But I would still love them.

This took the wind out of me, like when you land on a football when you are a kid. I suppose I was teary eyed for when my mother looked at me I saw her measuring my reaction. As if it wasn't clear that she had hurt me she went on.

Mom: Joe, what would you do if one of your kids told you they were gay?

Dad: Honey, if one of my kids was queer, it would break my heart. But I would love them. I would always love them.

My mother was watching me tear up. I could feel her come to a conclusion, a certainty and she was not backing off.

Mom: Why are you crying?

Me: Why do you think? Why are you doing this?

Mom: What am I doing to you?

Me: I don't know what it is, what are you doing, what do you want?

Mom: If one of my kids were gay, I wouldn't accept it but I would love them. I would love them. If one of my kids were gay, I wouldn't accept it but I would love them.

Me: Oh my god. Leave me alone.

Mom: Leave you alone?

Me: Yes, please let me go to bed.

Mom: If one of my kids were gay, I wouldn't accept it but I would love them.

I suppose the point in all of this was to break me, and it worked. I had been standing there for over an hour. I was mixed-up, drained. It was as if I was on a cliff and I was either going to be pushed off or about to jump off. I jumped.

Mom: If one of my kids were gay, I wouldn't accept it but I would love them.

Me: Then you better love me.

I headed for my room, and when I got to the stairs, I feel on my knees and sobbed. What had I done? Did I say I was gay? Did I just tell her I was gay? I ran up to my room and grabbed my things. Never unpacking was a wise choice. My mom was right behind me. She came right in and unlike me, who was afraid to go into her room she sat on my bed and lit another cigarette as I gathered my things and sobbed. She traveled with an ashtray so not to worry.

Mom: Where are you going?

Me: I don't know, out of here.

Mom: No you stay and talk to me!

Me: Talk? You are the only one talking.

Mom: Are you gay Jane?

Me: Yes Mom, I am.

Mom: Well I have some things to say.

Me: I'm leaving Mom. I get it. You love me, you won't accept it, and you won't approve and I chose this and I'm selfish and I will break Dad's heart.

Mom: Your father will go to his grave not knowing this!

Me: I'm leaving.

I went downstairs and passed my sister sitting up in her bed looking at me and crying. She came out of her room and hugged me and said, "I don't hate you." I went to the first floor with clickity clack following me down the stairs. Joanne stopped her on the second floor and was asking her questions. I sat down in Pat's wheelchair like we all did when we were talking to him when he was in bed. "I have to tell you something Pat," I said.

"No you don't Jane," he answered.

"Yes, I do, Pat. I hope you don't hate me…but…I'm gay."

"I know Jane, I heard the whole conversation, I don't hate you. Mom doesn't hate you," he said.

"Pat, she hates me, she has always hated me. I have to get out." I said, still crying.

"Jane, don't leave tonight, leave in the morning. If you need to go out, go to the diner with Joanne. If you leave tonight, Mom will feel like shit. Just don't go tonight, Ok?"

He was asking, but he knew I would do whatever he told me to.

"Ok," I said, and I went to the diner with my sister, a sophomore in high school and I told her she could ask me anything she wanted to know except for anything about sex. She said that was all she was really curious about. She asked me if I had a girlfriend and asked to see her picture. "Kinda pretty," she said. After we had coffee and hot cocoa, we went back home, and Joanne went to bed. I went into the kitchen and found my mother, having changed into her bathrobe, smoking. "I want to talk to you," she said. "Do you have a girlfriend?" I told her I did and asked if she wanted to see a picture.

"No, I do not!" she answered. "I want you to promise me one thing," she said.

"What's that mom?" I asked her.

"Promise me you won't ever bring someone into this life." I tilted my head at her, "What are you talking about?" I really didn't know what she meant at first.

"Just what I said, don't bring anyone into this life." She was clearly ending the conversation.

"Ok Mom. I'm going to go to sleep now. Goodnight."

The next morning I had convinced myself that if I just acted normal, like nothing had changed, my mom would see that I had not changed. So just as every other day I went down to her room and sat in her rocking chair as she smoked a cigarette and lounged on her bed. Just as every other morning, as I put my sneakers on I said, "How are you this morning mom?"

I finished tying my shoe and sat up in time to see the shoe before it hit my head. "How the hell do you think I am?" she asked. "Well you just threw a shoe at my head, I'm going to say, not so good."

I called my girlfriend about an hour later, and she said she would meet me at South Street in Philly in about six hours. She drove all the way from Long Island to get me; I had been waiting for three hours by the time she picked me up. I waited for over a year for my mother to ask me to come home.

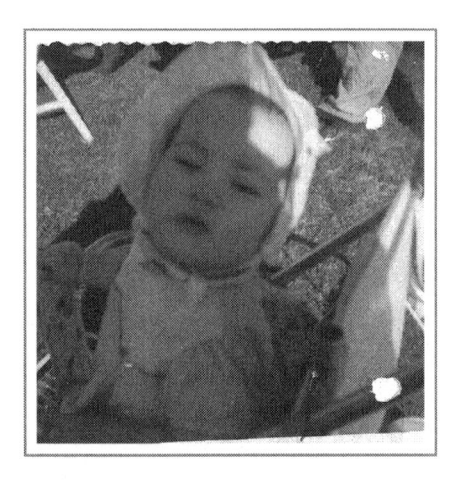

Author as infant planning the gay agenda!

CHAPTER 19

Sorry About Your Rainbow!

Recently I was selling tickets to a very nice woman who was supporting the arts here in Brattleboro. The woman had mentioned that she had been to our theater previously and on one occasion, both she and her husband were very upset by what they saw. When I asked what part of the show had bothered her I was not surprised that she said it was that the show had "homosexual content." She was right about that; I know because

I directed that show. The show was a collection of about eight scenes about couples in different stages of their relationships. Six of these scenes were heterosexual, one scene was a lesbian couple, and one scene was about two gay young men. Each scene was handled the same way with the actors "acting" the parts and trying to be real about the situations. I was extremely proud of the group, as they had taken on topics and scenarios far beyond their years.

So here I was, face to face with a woman who had had a very disappointing night at the theater because of me. I mentioned that I had directed the show, and she just nodded. For a moment, I felt bad for her. Racists are at least aware that they are talking to someone of a race they dislike. I almost felt like I should have worn my "I'm a lesbo" hat so she could have curbed her speech. I couldn't say anything to her for a variety of reasons, the foremost being that I just felt bad for her small world and I truly felt that her generation will probably (hopefully) be the last where the dislike of gays is something to be proud of rather than ashamed. So that happened, and late into the day I was still upset by it. I know I can't go back in time and say something wise and eye opening to her, but the incident reminded me of a conversation I had probably twenty years ago.

I had come to visit my parents at their beach rental one summer, and another person (who shall remain nameless) was visiting as well. This person was a couple of years younger than me and had married my brother. (Still no name)

She was smashed when she stumbled in the door around 3:00 am, ruining my perfect night of watching a Twilight Zone Marathon. We chatted for a few seconds, and I started to feel like there was something on her mind. I also felt that the "something" might be something I didn't want to hear.

BINGO!

This is what I heard.

"iuztahafareighbostikronmycarannowihadtatakeitoff."

Naturally I said, "What?"

After a few repeats, I realized that she was saying that she had a rainbow sticker on her car but that she had to take it off.

"Why did you take it off?" I asked, knowing the answer was going to be good!

"casidonwanpeepilthinkinimgay!"

This, of course, meant, "because, I don't want people thinking I am gay!"

This was a silly thought because if she had been literally covered in "dyke" tattoos, nobody would believe it. This girl was straight!

She followed her tale of woe with a tirade about how I had ruined her rainbow, and she wanted to know why!

I was laughing too hard twenty years ago, but now I'd like to answer that for her. It's like this. We gays all got together to decide what to ruin by claiming it as our own. It came down to the Rainbow, or the Unicorn. I voted with the majority, and we chose to ruin the rainbow. The unicorn was deemed too fucking gay!

So there, I answered your question, long after you asked it, but there it is.

So I'm sorry 'bout your rainbow, but you'll always have your unicorn, I noticed that sticker stayed on your car.

CHAPTER 20

Summer of Love

After I had realized I was gay and well before my parents caught on, I was to be a camp counselor at an all-girls sleep away camp. I was going to be working in the theater department. It was such an exciting time for my sexual self since I had just figured it out and I couldn't believe I was headed to the deep woods to be away from my gay friends for the summer. I would have no one to talk to.

I arrived at the camp after endless hours on Greyhounds and a very long ride through the woods late at night. The camp was not yet ready, and the lights were not even working in the bunks. I can't think of a person more ill suited for being in the woods without light than me at that time in my life. The dark scared me; the woods scared me, I scared me. A big part of having panic attacks for me was that I always imagined in my mind that I would embarrass or humiliate other people and myself. I remember one of those first nights when we all sat around the camp kitchen talking, and there was a wall of knives. I was feeling anxious, and my mind wandered. Within seconds I had taken a fear of the knives and turned myself into a mass murderer. I was so worried I would hurt someone and become a terrible person. I often wonder what the things are that make us so afraid of being wicked? Church perhaps, nature/nurture—something.

So much time wasted worrying.

One day while helping set up the camp a busload of counselors arrived, and I wondered if I might find a gay guy to talk to among them. I didn't. What I did find were around thirty beautiful, athletic and super gay looking women. I would like to think I looked poised, but I think the passing out was probably a sign I was overwhelmed. "Kid in a candy store," comes to mind but I wasn't a kid, and this was not candy. I was a lesbian in a camp full of female counselors! Life was so much more than good; it was gay! I fell in love every time I turned around.

I first fell in love with a woman who turned out to be there with her girlfriend, but in that day, people didn't talk about being gay at all. There were hints, like rainbow flags, earrings in only one ear, women kissing you. These were subtle, but I was pretty quick catching on.

The first woman I fell in love with had the most unbelievable blue eyes. Eyes are a soft spot for me, so are arms, legs, hair, ears, smiles, faces, in general, bodies, come to think of it; women. Yep, it's women. The blue-eyed beauty with the unbelievable eyes was wearing colored contacts. This was my first broken heart. I moved on the next day. I then fell in love with an Ivy League juggler. She was funny and very smart and she gave the best back rubs. I didn't find out until I got my lesbian handbook, but backrubs are lesbian foreplay. I was terrified to tell her I was gay and for weeks we had the most beautiful affair, but she didn't know it until the summer was over and we caught up over Thanksgiving break. There were a few moments, usually late at night when we would canoe out to an island and lie there looking at the beautiful Maine sky when I thought that this was the best life could get. I might not have been too far off.

One day when she was not at breakfast I went to her bunk to wake her, and she was not feeling well. I kidded her that I would make her get up, and we ended up wrestling. There, for what was probably just a short moment, but felt like a whole separate life, our faces were inches from each other. I wanted to kiss her so desperately but was so worried that I was reading her wrong and would ruin our friendship. I wish I had because now I know that there is only one thing that could have been happening, and I missed it. I think the intensity of what we felt was one reason that we both moved on to other obsessions as this one was causing so much confusion.

I turned, unknowingly to the first woman's girlfriend. Let's say they were less than totally honest with one another. This was the first woman that I had not known to be gay who made herself clear to me.

There was a counselor's hut that the off-duty counselors would hang out in when their bunks were in for the night. Many nights this woman would be sitting there, and she would look into my eyes and smile and I would melt. She wrote me notes that said things like, "Let's meet out near the lake later," and I would hyperventilate. One night she leaned into me and said, "You have bedroom eyes." A worldly chick, I said, "I'm not tired." She laughed at what she thought was the joke I made. I later found out that I was (again) confused. Only once did I have the nerve to meet her at the lake and we took a canoe out. (I know, canoes should be registered with Lesbian Homoland Security.) We canoed out to the middle of the lake, and she asked me if I wanted to kiss her. I was so scared this was a trap or a trick, and I just said coolly, "Shut up!"

"Okay," she said and took all her clothes off and jumped in the water. I was speechless and so happy. "If you change your mind, jump in."

Without missing a beat, I leapt into the water.

"You really could have taken your clothes off first you know," she mentioned.

"Yeah, but I'm shy," I replied.

"Yeah, you are shy!" she laughed. This is something I find to be baffling to some people. I am a loud and silly person, but there are some situations where I actually do have shyness about me. Sex, kissing, love, those are the situations. I swam over to her, sinking, as my jeans were really heavy now.

"You're going to drown," she said. I kissed her and then did begin to sink. She pulled me back up, and we laughed and she warned me that I really might drown if I didn't get back in the boat. I said I wanted to kiss her again, and then I would get back in the boat. We compromised, and she said we could kiss again after I was no longer sinking. I climbed into the boat and helped her in. She sat next to me, and we kissed for at least a half hour and then it was clear that we needed to stop or not stop but, either way, we needed to get out of the canoe. We paddled the boat in; she got dressed, and I walked her back to her bunk. In complete darkness except for the stars I kissed her goodnight and thought I would die a very happy camper.

I turned around, and her girlfriend was standing there.

"Hi," I said.

"Shit," my kissing partner said. I was not sure what was going on, but it turned out that this was my first experience with crazy lesbian jealousy and freak-outs. "Have a nice ride on the lake?" her girlfriend asked.

"Yeah," I said.

"I'm not asking you," she said.

"Oh," I replied.

Things started adding up when I looked at kissing girl and back at contact-wearing girl and saw a look that told me I was in the middle.

"Um, I don't know what's going on but I'm going to head to bed," I said, sure that this was the end of my involvement.

"No, don't go," kissing girl said.

"It's ok, I should go, " I said, hoping to get out of this before it got weirder.

Contact-wearing girl was very happy to see me go, and I was less than pleased that kissing girl had not let me know that I was an unknowing participant in an unkind experience for her girlfriend. I remained friendly but removed from both of them, and they remained all over the place for the rest of the summer. I next found myself in love with a much older woman; she was twenty-eight, and I—a mere nineteen—was smitten. She was a former college athlete who was now a gym teacher in California.

No jokes, please. She had the body of a former college athlete who was now a gym teacher, and I was pretty obvious in my admiration for it. She figured me out quickly and was more than encouraging. She was older and had moved on from the stage I was in, where every kiss was a possible marriage and a sacred event that should only happen when carefully choreographed to Holly Near or Cris Williamson music.

Her stage was more along the lines of a woman who liked sex, a lot. I was such a prude that this approach to the sacred meeting of Sapphic souls offended me. I'm joking; I totally went for it and had a thoroughly wonderful time.

I would have been insulted by how quickly she was moving on, but someone else had caught my eye. The woman I was captivated by was physically the cutest person I had ever seen. That may have been what initially drew me to her, but I quickly found out that she had a really great sense of humor, and I loved that almost as much as everything else about women. I soon found out that we also shared a deep and recent hurt with one another. I had a few years before lost my brother David, and she had very recently lost her brother, I think in a car accident, and came right to camp after the funeral. She was still in shock I think, and we spent many nights by a fire talking about life and death and our brothers. Nothing romantic ever happened with her but what did was so welcome. I had found no one until then to talk to who understood my loss. Summer of love complete!

(For the sake of their privacy, all women in this picture are disguised. That's me in the middle of the Jodies.)

PART FOUR

Hired Hand

CHAPTER 21

Procurer of Broadway Show Tickets

THE THEATRE

When we moved into NYC we were all quickly employed by TicketCall, a Broadway ticket selling company that took up a whole floor in the McGraw Hill Building on 43rd St. There were about seventy phone agents working in little commune-like areas that had stations taking up half of the floor that seated eight agents each. With our newly minted diplomas in Theater we were the perfect ironic nobodies to sell tickets to see other people on stage who were living their dream.

We followed a script so at the beginning of every call we would say, "Hello, this is TicketCall, what show would you like to see?" Usually this opening remark was met with a declarative statement like, "We want to see *My One and Only!*" Sometimes the customer would be a bit flummoxed and say, "I don't know what do you recommend?" Only one time did I hear what I would call a Declarative Nonsensical response: "I want two tickets to *Cats: Now and Forever!*" This was an understandable mistake for a Broadway show newbie so I explained. "Actually ma'am, the show is simply called "Cats."

"Do I sound like a simpleton to you?" she asked.

"No ma'am." I said, because she was proving quite complicated.

"I have seen 'Cats' seven times already!" This seemed excessive to me, I couldn't get through Cats once! Everyone was dressed like a Cat, I'm not even kidding!

"Pardon me ma'am, I misunderstood, I thought you said you did want to see *Cats,* my mistake, what should would you like to get tickets for?"

I could hear her take a deep breath like she couldn't believe she had to deal with a moron agent.

"Listen carefully, I want to go see *Cats: Now and Forever!*"

I admit I was getting a bit impatient. "Ma'am, you just told me you don't want tickets to *Cats.*"

"I do not want tickets to *Cats!* I want tickets to *Cats: Now and Forever!* Do you understand me?"

No, I did not understand her at all, not one bit.

"Ma'am, TicketCall is currently selling tickets to *Cats* at the Wintergreen Theater. We have no show called *Cats Now and Forever.*"

"I just saw the commercial for it ten minutes ago! Are you telling me I'm wrong?"

I quickly checked with a co-worker about this cats now and forever commercial. "Ma'am I see what happened. The theater has been airing a new advertisement campaign for the show *Cats.*"

She would not be swayed. And so our exchange continued.

Agent is **BOLD**

Unshakable determined woman is REGULAR

"It's for *Cats: Now and Forever.*"

"Actually that is the name of the campaign. They are saying that *Cats*, the show is a play for all time, that it's playing now, and they hope forever."

"I have not seen it yet, I can't say if it will play forever. I don't know if it's as good as *Cats*."

"Ma'am, there is not a show called *Cats: Now and Forever*, it is the same show, it's called *Cats*."

"Young lady, are you refusing to sell me tickets to *Cats now and forever?*"

"I am not refusing ma'am, it is impossible."

"Why, are you an idiot?"

Whoa! This was getting a bit mean spirited. **"No ma'am, I'm not."**

"Then sell me the tickets, any Friday night, as soon as possible, two tickets, the best seats possible."

"For *Cats: Now and Forever*?"

"Yes, do you think you can manage to handle that?

"You got it! Let's see, you could go this Friday evening, will that work for you?"

"Yes, finally!"

After the credit card is used and the tickets confirmed by the computer, we had to do a quick review of the order and for fear of being overheard by the supervisor I had to whisper this review script.

"Ma'am, I'm pleased to tell you that you have purchased tickets for this Friday evenings performance of... *Cats*...at the Winter Garden Theater, 1634 Broadway. The total cost of your tickets is ...

"Wait, you said "*Cats*."

"Yes ma'am I did."

"But I wanted...."

"Fine, "Ma'am, I'm pleased to tell you that you have purchased tickets for this Friday evenings performance of *Cats: Now and Forever*, at the Winter Garden Theater, 1634 Broadway. The total cost of your tickets is $75.50 and has been charged to your Visa. We are happy that you chose to call TicketCall for your Broadway Ticket needs and we hope you enjoy *Cats*!"

"What?"

"Now and Forever."

"I hope it's good."

"I'm sure it will be! Goodbye."

The best part of working at TicketCall was that I was with so many friends. The best shifts for me were when I sat right next to my roomies. During one shift when Tommy was next to me the calls were slow. I heard Tom having a difficult time on the phone and he looked like he was about ready to shoot himself. I plugged into the extra spot to listen to the call and see what was happening. The woman was clearly elderly and a big 42nd Street in fan. She was driving Tom nuts by asking him to repeatedly review the order she had made. The woman finally said, "Is there anything else I need to know?" and I said in my best Tom voice,

"Madam I love you." Tom looked horrified and pulled the plug on me. I laughed like I had just done the funniest thing in the world; Tom did not. I could hear the woman on the phone, "What did you say?" and poor Tom's response, "I said that you have ordered two tickets to *42nd Street*." After wrapping up the phone call Tom turned to me and just glared. "One day, something terrible will happen, you will wonder who did it, then it will occur to you. It will have been me." This made me laugh even more. I assumed with that kind of cryptic warning that the payback would come in a few years when I had forgotten the threat. I was wrong. That night at around 2:00 I had a dream I was falling. Turned out it was not a dream. Tom had launched me off the side of the loft bed, at least 6 feet off the ground and I plunged to the floor. As soon as I realized what had happened I laughed the hardest I had ever laughed in my life. Tom has always had this ability to make me almost vomit laughing. A charming image I know. I crawled back up the stairs into the bed and asked him, "Even?" Without looking at me Tom smirked and said, "Yes, dyke, now go to bed." I laughed some more.

When people think "Christmas," they think overpriced theater tickets! Or at least TicketCall thought so. Employees in their first year had to work Christmas Eve and Christmas Day. As Christmas approached I went to the office to ask for an exception to this Christmas rule. I thought I had a pretty good reason and explained to the boss.

"I would really appreciate it if I could go home, my brother is very ill and it may be his last Christmas." I awaited the condolences and the obvious permission to miss work that was forthcoming when my boss said. "Hey Jane, if we gave everyone who has a 'dying brother' off for Christmas where would we be, who would work?"

I was not sure if this guy was yanking on me or not, "Are you serious?" I asked.

"Very." he said.

"Come on, are you really telling me that everyone out there has a brother that is dying?"

He looked at me and smiled, "Well they probably have as much of a dying brother as you have, you forget I see you actresses coming in here with your stories…" I stood up to leave and said, "Sir, if there are people so lame that they would say such a thing when it was not true then I don't know what to say other than I am telling the truth, I wish I were lying, and I have to go home for Christmas."

"If you don't work Christmas Eve and Christmas Day, don't bother coming in ever again."

CHAPTER 22

Governess

The very first job I ever had, not counting combing the fringe on the rugs in our hallway before my parents threw a party, was babysitting.

I was twelve and I babysat for a couple of "professionals in Philadelphia." I didn't know what they were being professional about but it was something that I had never heard before. There were no professionals in Havertown that I knew of. This couple had two youngins, a boy and girl, seven and five years old. These kids were easy, feed them, send them to bed, and look around their parents' room. If you learn nothing else from my experiences, learn this: your babysitter will look around your bedroom because they will, they may not want to, but they will be drawn to look like a fat kid to chocolate, that is also from my experience. One night when the kids were off in dreamland I strolled into their room found some stuff sitting around, like a book or two—they were smart!

I saw a book on the nightstand that looked neat so I walked around the bed to see what it was. I was distracted by what looked like a kid's toy sticking out from underneath the bed. I picked it up to put it back in the kids room and thought, "What kind of parents get their kid a toy that looks like a penis?" Why would anyone have an item like this? Did they have fake boobs and fake ears under the bed too? Then I wondered if the husband was lacking a penis. Could that happen? Could it fall off? Vietnam? Then I realized that they *did* something with this! It was clear to me then that I was in Satan's house! Good people did not have such items! I didn't know what to make of this except that these people were perhaps witches, possibly demons, possibly never to be my employers again.

As I stood trying to figure out if I should put it back where I found it or to throw up, the little girl woke up and called for me. I threw the penile element under the bed and ran to her room. "What are you doing up? I wasn't in your parents room."

She told me she had to go pee but was afraid to go to the bathroom because the light was not on. I walked her to the bathroom and waited outside for her and then walked her back. "Can you tell me a story to get me to sleep?" little Cindy Lou Who asked. "Sure." So I told her a story, mostly a silly tale of a bear and a raccoon and hijinks galore. "How's the story so far?" She thought about it and said, "It was okay."

"Hey now, I'm not finished, what does the story need? Funnier? Scarier?"

"It's not scary at all." Challenge on. "Okay, I can make it scarier!" This was a terrible idea. What happened was quick and vague. Somehow the funny bear ended outside her window banging to get in. Then the tears started. "Why is the bear trying to get in?" I felt terrible, this was all going so bad so fast. "No, no, it's not really a bear, it's…your dad, he's just wearing a costume, and he takes the head of the costume off and it's your dad! Yeah, Dad!" The sobbing continued to get louder and faster, "Why did my Daddy take his head off?"

"No no, not his head, the bear's head!"

"My daddy took a bear's head off, why?"

I was exhausted and guilt ridden, I just wanted to tell her a sweet bedtime story and instead sent her into a breakdown.

The parents pulled in a couple hours later and asked how it went.

"Great! No problems!"

Of course I couldn't look them in the eye because one of them did or did not have a penis and their daughter was probably damaged forever because of the dad/bear story.

They never called me again. Years later I heard they divorced.

I couldn't help but blame the penis.

CHAPTER 23

Telecommunications Professional

Way back when phones were attached to walls and there was no voice mail, answering services were relied on by everyone— not just doctors so you could find out if the doctor who was on call was the one at the practice you did not want to deliver your child. Doctors, lawyers, plumbers, oil companies, and loads of others paid to have live operators take the calls they couldn't get to, and then let them know who called. This was so long ago there wasn't even regular mail. People just wrote notes and attached them with a pin to people they thought might be going in the direction they wanted their note to go.

I worked at the answering service two blocks from my house throughout high school, and when home from college for summers or short breaks. Every kind of doctor had the service, and before their staff went home they would call us and tell us who was on call and when to call or beep.

We got every kind of weird call you can imagine and some that I never would have imagined or believed had they not been calls I took.

Dr. Madagun was an OB-GYN, and I was extremely squeamish about answering this line. But sometimes it would get busy and before you knew it you had accidentally answered it.

Me answering the OB-GYN line by accident: "Dr. Madagun's answering service."

Caller: Um, hi, I'm a patient of Dr. Madagun's, and I have a little problem.

Me, Wanting to Get Off Phone: Okay, if I can get your name and the nature of the problem, I can call the doctor.
Shy Caller: Well, I don't really want to say.

(Keep in mind I am a very young sixteen-year-old who knows nothing of the ways of the OB-GYN.)

Me, Glad I Won't Know What's Wrong: Miss, I can only tell you that I most likely want to hear what is wrong less than you don't want to say what's wrong, but I can't call the doctor without telling him something.

Shy Caller, Getting Loose: Okay, could you just tell him it's tampon-related?

Me, Unsure of What the Hell That Meant: Yes, I can do that.

Shy, Confusing Caller: Well, a tampon has gone missing.

Me, Now Bothered: Pardon me?

Not-Shy-Anymore Oversharing Caller: I had a tampon in, and now I can't find it.

(This was like telling me a submarine fell into outer space because as good Catholic girls, we didn't use tampons until college, when our mothers didn't know what we did, so she could have said the tampon combusted and I would not have been surprised.)

Me, Now Wrapping This Call Up: So you lost it, okay, I'll tell him.

Caller with No Boundaries: Well, what happened was—

Me, Losing Blood Flow to Brain: No, ma'am, that's plenty, I don't need to know anything else.

Caller, Clearly Intent on Making Me Pass Out: I had a tampon in, heavy flow, and my boyfriend and I were messing around, and—

Me, Wanting the Lord to Let This Cup Pass Me By: No, please, I have all I need.

Caller, Kissing and Telling: So we had sex.

Me, Trying to Unhear: No.

Caller, Gone Wild: And I think he got the tampon lost in my uterus.

Me, Horrified: What?

Caller, Repeating Nausea-Inducing Details: In my uterus.

Me, Losing It: God, no. Stop. Let me call the doctor.

Caller, Seeking Comfort: Do you think it's in my uterus?

Me, Wanting to Go Home: I honestly don't know if a tampon could be in your uterus or not. But I can tell the doctor that your tampon went missing, and he can go looking for it.

Caller: I think it's in my uterus.

Me, Finished Talking: I will tell him to look there first.

CHAPTER 24

Broadway House Hotel

After I lost my job at TicketCall, because I made that funny joke about a sick brother, I got a job at a hotel that had recently been purchased by a company that owned bathhouses all over the country. Bathhouses were being shut down and so the company was branching out to hotels.

When they purchased the Broadway House Hotel it was not without its little problems. The hotel had originally been a women's boarding house. Women rented a room and shared a kitchen and bathrooms with the whole floor. Imagine a hotel with six floors of young Broadway Hopefuls, that's what most of them were when they took residence in the hotel in the 1940's. Now imagine these women forty years later. Still hopeful, but youth was long gone, the average woman there was between sixty and eighty years old. The owners' plan was to wait these women out and floor by floor, renovate and make the hotel a real hotel.

At this time there were only two floors of actual transient hotel guests. It was a very cheap place to stay in New York City and there was a good reason for it. There were very few fancy hotels in NYC where—while checking in—you had an extraordinarily high chance of spotting a naked octogenarian running after the manager with a broom and smacking him upside the head while yelling, "I know what you are! You are a sodomite!" While technically she may have been correct it should be mentioned that she was politically incorrect for stating such and also, she continued to be naked. This woman was a very feisty one. There were so many women there that we only knew them by their room number. Every floor had at least one woman that was worthy of her own psych ward. The woman I knew as 509 was probably sixty-five years old and she looked like a man who didn't really want to be in drag, because if a guy wants to he will look fabulous. She looked like a man who wore women's clothes as a means of hiding from a previous family. She would come down to the reservation desk every night and ask me what time it was, I would tell her and then she would call the desk as soon as she returned to her room and ask again. Eventually I got very tired of this and put a clock in her mailbox, it seemed that maybe she needed one; I wasn't trying to be rude. She didn't like the clock. I know because she brought it down at 4:00 when I came to work and waited until she had my attention. I assumed she was going to thank me for the clock. She didn't. She walked over to the desk, placed in on the counter, and then tipped it ever so gently into my coffee mug below. She didn't say a word, turned around and went upstairs and called me to ask what time it was.

"I am sorry if I offended you, I thought maybe you needed a clock."

"Uh-huh, is that what you thought?" she asked.

"Yes," I said.

"What time is it?" she said.

"Really?" I replied, "I just gave you a clock!"

"I didn't ask for a clock did I?" she yelled.

"No, but I don't understand why you don't want one, then you wouldn't have to call me four times a night," I said.

"Are you mopping a floor?" she asked me.

"No." I answered.

"Then you aren't working," she said and hung up. Everyone has a different idea of what work is I guess. According to her I was not working, because I was not mopping. Fair enough. I told my co-worker about what happened when he came in at 11 to relieve me.

"Oh, 509, orange hands?" he asked.

"Yeah, why are her hands orange, I've been meaning to ask you," I asked.

"Iodine. She soaks her hands in iodine every day," he informed me.

"Why?" I asked.

"Why!" he said, "You're funny."

He did have a point, asking why about most of what happened there was senseless.

The rent for these women was very low because of rent control and the fact that they had moved in before the colonies broke off from England. One woman, 316 came in one day crying, she was at eighty-seven years old. I knew because she began every sentence with a declaration of her age.

"Oh Jane, you won't believe what happened to this eighty-seven year old woman today!" she said.

"What happened, why are you crying?" I asked her.

"This eighty-seven year old woman's social security check is all used up in one day!" she declared.

"Well how did that happen?" I asked.

"I accidentally gave all of this eighty-seven year old's money to the church. What am I going to do, I can't pay my rent!" she asked me.

I looked up her rent and I can say without a doubt that this was the only time in my life that I had enough money in my pocket to pay for another person's monthly rent in NYC. Four dollars and eighteen cents! We walked to the church the next day before my shift and I asked them for her money back. That did not go well, but she also didn't go back.

405 was a sneaky little woman of many wigs. She always wore a raincoat and one of her blond wigs when going out. One day in the spring 405 came down to the front desk and told me she was going to the St. Patty's day parade. I told her that it sounded exciting. She said it was going to be because someone was going to try to shoot the Cardinal. I asked her why she thought that and she pointed to her wig, which now that attention was brought to it looked a little lumpy.

"I have a gun in my wig, " she said smiling.

"What?" I asked.

"A gun, a good one too, I'm gonna shoot him up in the head under that stupid hat," she said.

"You really don't like him huh?" I asked, playing along because obviously she wasn't really carrying a gun or going to shoot the cardinal!

"Well, I'm off, I guess I won't see you again!" and she was off. After a few minutes I wondered if I should tell someone, just because she was a bit loopy and she could hurt someone with her wig if she tried hard enough. I looked out the window and there was a cop so I yelled out to him to come over to talk to me. I told him what had happened and he seemed not at all concerned. A few hours later the cops escorted 405 into the lobby, sans wig. She came over and stood at the counter.

"Some asshole ratted me out! Can you believe that?" she asked.

"Nooooo!" I said, "Why?"

"Ah, I don't know, anyway, my gun wasn't loaded so I don't have to go to jail tonight, but I have to go to court tomorrow. Do you want to come and be a character witness?"

"I would, but I have two jobs and I have to work both tomorrow but please tell me how it goes!"

"I just want my wig back. They are keeping the gun," she said, at peace with the decision.

"Probably a good idea don't you think?" I asked her.

"I don't know. I guess I don't need it anymore, the cardinal got away," she said.

"Tough break, maybe next time?" I said. She shrugged and said she had to get her rest for court. She got her wig back and it looked better without the lump.

By far the most interesting and bizarre interactions took place with 811. 811 was easily seventy-five and about four and a half feet tall. She wore fur coats and looked curiously like Yoda. She talked to me every night. Almost every night she would mention that were I not so fat, I would be pretty. Sweet woman. She was really frank; she would just put it out there.

"I was thinking, you would be pretty if you lost some of that fat," she'd say.

"Hmmm. Thank you?" I would say.

"You're welcome," she would reply. She often spoke of the goings on at the hotel that I had no knowledge of, most of which happened over night according to her. There was a tiger that lived in the room above her with an animal trainer but because they didn't want to get caught they only trained at three in the morning. John F. Kennedy had been hiding on the fourth floor since the assassination attempt. I admit I did find that one shocking, I was also curious as to who was tending to that head wound. She often hinted at the illegal behaviors of my employers but didn't want to tell me what they had done because I had to work for them.

A few nights after one of her rants on how terrible my bosses were my manager came in and he was furious. I asked him what was wrong and he said, "811."

"Oh, what did she do?" I asked. "I've been in court all day because of her," he told me.

"What happened?" I asked.

"Well, you see, she filed a suit against us for all of the things she says we have been doing to her," he said.

"I didn't know you were doing anything to her," I said.

"Oh yeah, guess what we've been doing, and you are involved too, just so you know," he said. "First, you need to stop climbing into her closet through a hole in the back and making microscopic cuts in her furs with a razor that only she can see," he said to me.

"Are you serious?" I asked.

"Sure am!" he said, "and that's only what you have done. Guess what I did, last night even?" he asked me.

"Did you repair the microscopic cuts I made?" I asked, hopeful that someone would cover up for me.

"Nope, I took an envelope and filled it with cocaine and slipped it under her door so her rabbit, which, by the way, she isn't supposed to have in her room, would get high!" he said.

"Are you telling me you didn't do that?" I asked.

"It's such a waste of time and money and city resources, and you know what, the judge asked me 'how do you plead?' How do I plead? Well I lost my shit and I told him that if I had an envelope full of cocaine the last thing I would do with it would be to give it to a rabbit!" he was still very riled up.

"That makes sense," I said.

"I got fined $50.00 for disrespecting the court!" he said.

Later that night after my manager went home 811 came in and told me that I should stop breaking into her closet, she was onto me and that if I just lost some weight I would get a date and lose interest in her furs. Yoda was right, I had to stop the microscopic cutting, and it was getting out of hand.

CHAPTER 25

Stray Cat Strut at the Answering Service

Another incident from the answering service that has always stayed with me was an incident involving Martini and Rossi. There was some wine or other alcoholic drink named Martini and Rossi and not by coincidence our office cats were named Martini and Rossi. I had always been afraid of cats, possibly because my mother routinely told us of how a cat had attacked her during a childhood vacation, and how she was convinced that the cat was trying to claw her eyes out.

My mother hated cats, didn't want to talk about cats, and was very wary of anyone that would have, or consider having a cat as a pet.

I was determined to find out for myself about cats and while out with my dad picked up what turned out to be a wild barn cat. It tried to eat my head. After that I was firmly in my mom's cat camp. The cats at the answering service usually remained in the back office so I was not usually overly concerned with their existence. One night I was working with one other person and I did not know this woman very well but she did strike me as a person whose elevator did not go to the top floor, if you get my subtle drift. This woman was, I'm sure, well intentioned and kind at heart, but she made some questionable choices. On this particular night, the phones were slow and we spent a lot of time looking out at a massive rainstorm. The rain was coming down so hard it sounded like rocks against the window. Our two cats had recently become the parents to a litter of six kittens. The fact that the parents were siblings was slightly worrisome to me on a moral and practical level. Firstly, does one say "Aunt Mommy" or "Mommy Aunt" and would they refer to each other, were they able to speak as "Sister Wife" and "Brother Husband?" There was one kitten that bore the brunt of the ill thought romance and she was, sadly, born with a multitude of issues. Martini, the mother cat, was very protective of the kittens, as cats are known to be, but particularly protective of the kitten which the bosses, not me, named "dopeycat." The weather was getting pretty intimidating and you could hardly see across the road when my co-worker, whom I will call "half-wit," only because I have no memory of calling her anything other than a string of curses. Half-wit notices a cat outside the office hiding under the awning. This cat looks a mess, possibly because it is in the worst storm ever or equally possible because it is clearly a stray. Half-wit says, "Hey, that cat needs to get out of this storm, my my my!" To which I said, "No freakin way you can let that cat in here! There are kittens and no!" I did not feel good about this at all and thought I had made myself clear when Half-wit walked over to the door and let the cat in. Immediately Rossi, the father cat pounced into the room and made the most hideous shriek while getting wide eyed at the cat/rat that Half-wit had let in, immediately after that, Martini ran in and made her own war cry. Calls kept coming in and I answered them until Rossi jumped across my desk and then chased the stray rat. Stray-rat-cat landed on my desk and I screamed. Martini was chasing her and it looked like that the stray, while glaring into my eyes was evaluating my value as a hiding place. The stray rat lunged at me and I quickly dove into the bathroom and locked the door. Half-wit yelled, "Hey, come out here and help me with these cats! My my my." Now Rossi and the Stray and Martini were having the kind of catfight you hear in an alley four stories below you and you say to yourself "God am I glad I'm nowhere near that!" "Nope, not coming out," I said, "you did this, you deal with it." I was lucky I was in the bathroom because the cats fighting in front of me made me pee. I was terrified and Half-wit thought that was so funny. "Oh my, are you scared of cats? How silly!" she said. She was actually laughing. "You won't be laughing when those cats rip your stupid eyes out you senseless, stupid, idiotic, dumb head person!" I said, fairly confident that she would have her eyes ripped out and that would terminate the laughter. About an hour went by before the rain stopped and she let the trespasser cat back outside. "You can come out now chicken!" Half-wit said. I came out and was stunned at what I saw. "What the hell? Is that blood?" I asked, a silly question because if it wasn't blood then the Half-wit had painted the office while I hid. "A little" Half-wit said. "A little? Holy shit, are the cats dead?" I asked. "Nooooooooo, I just let it back out," Half-wit said. "Not that cat, Martini and Rossi!" I said. "Oh, I don't know, they went in the office. A week later the mother, Martini died of injuries sustained in the fight that was 100% avoidable had a moron not let a stray cat in the office. With the mother now deceased we were charged with answering calls on the oldest pbx switchboard in the world, think Lily Tomlin's Ernestine set up, while bottle-feeding six kittens. Funny thing about kittens, when one cries they all cry. I think the people calling in must have thought we ran our answering service out of a vacant cage at the SPCA. The cats grew up and the one the office kept was "dopeycat." She really was very sweet and loving as a kitten but she grew into a very aggressive cat. For whatever reason this cat hated my feet and every time I came to work she would come out of hiding and try to bite my feet. The biting was bad but the hiss/gargle that accompanied the attack were simultaneously scary and ridicules. I found out if you giggled while being attacked by such a cat that they would grow incensed and declare war on your person. This answering service experience with cats is why, even now, I will not be shoeless around cats. I also wear glasses with no prescription to protect my eyes and earplugs so I can't hear the fights. I have also invented the world's first and most likely finest cat proof panic room. I am beginning to wonder if this incident had a lasting impact on me.

PART FIVE

Adulthood & Mommy Time

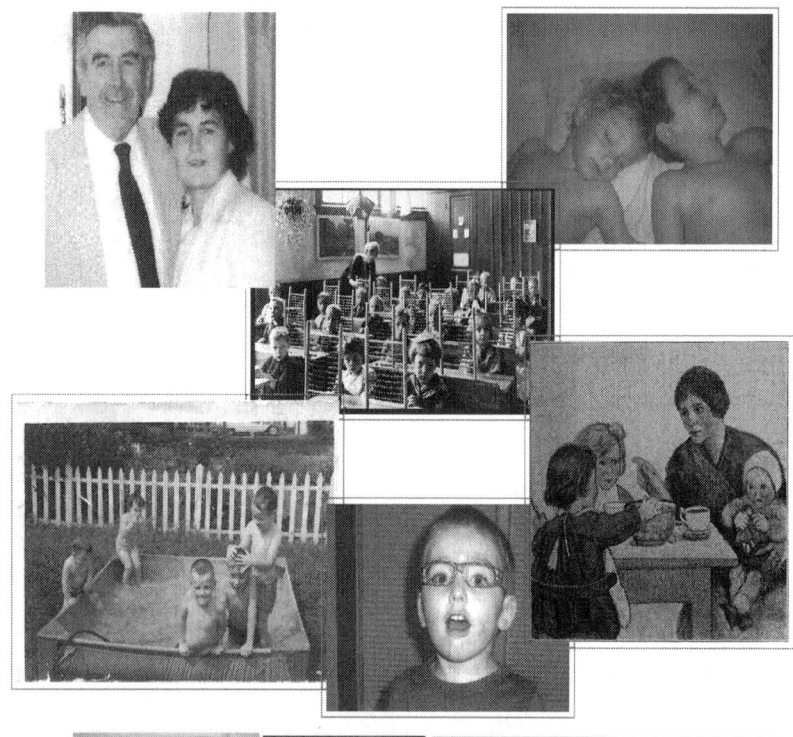

CHAPTER 26

If I Should Die.

I wrote this in 2002, when my mother Dolores died. Sammy was the only child we had at that time. No offense Max, and know that it all applies to you as well, as you and Sam are my two most loved boys in the world.

Sammy,

When my mommy got very sick she couldn't talk much and I wonder what she would have said if she could have. In case that ever happens to me there are some things I want you to know. I love you with all my heart and the only wish that I have is that you are happy. I want you to try everything that you dream of doing. Don't be afraid to do things that scare you. In fact, you have to do the things that scare you, (within reason) because it makes you grow and makes you strong. If I were no longer able to tell you what I felt about you I would always want you to remember these things about me.

I saw people I love die very young and it taught me many things:

Life is short.

Be glad for what you have.

I have lived a long life by comparison to many.

I never want to outlive my boy.

I have never loved so much, so deeply and so joyously as I love you.

You have made me smile every day of your life.

What I want you to know about your Momma,

She is a wonderful person and a wonderful mother.

She loves you as much as I do.

I love her.

She loves me.

We both adore you.

What I want you to know about yourself.

You are so smart and so clever,

You are funny.

You are loving, sweet and very kind.

You make me so proud and happy and you are the best thing I have had a hand in creating. I love you with all my heart and hope more that anything that you have a wonderful, adventurous, beautiful fun exciting life and that eternity finds me close to you and your momma.

I used to sing to you a song from a book we read to you.

What I sang was

"I love you forever,

I like you for always,

As long as I'm living

My baby you'll be."

I have held you many times memorizing how peaceful and beautiful and magnificent life can be, memorizing what it feels like to hold you close to me. I have memorized that feeling and know that I can think of that feeling always and be reminded of why I was born. I was born to be your mommy and it has been the greatest experience of my life. If I were to die today I would be so sad for leaving you and know that you would miss me but I wouldn't want you to be sad because I would want you to know that I knew I was lucky to be your mommy and that I am grateful to god for sending you to me. I asked god that you outlive me. I have also asked that I live to see you graduate from high school, college, see your wedding etc. I don't want to be pushy and ungrateful. I know the things I have been given and I thank god for you every day. If I have to leave you I promise that I will always look after you and want you to know that I will always be in your heart and holding you in mine.

CHAPTER 27

Hazed and Confused

In 2000, we welcomed Sam into our family when the doctors lovingly cut him out of me. Shortly after that beautiful event, we realized that if we stayed in Columbus, Ohio, where we were living when we had him, and something were to happen to me, any nutcake from my family, and there are many, could have claimed a right to raise Sam over Sharon. Sharon and I made a deal that we would both search for jobs in Vermont and the first to get a job would take it.

Although Sharon and I had met in Pennsylvania, we had later moved to Columbus, where Sharon got her J.D. from Ohio State.

(Note: My mother always told my sister and I to marry lawyers or doctors. When I mentioned that Sharon was getting a law degree and that I would be doing as she suggested, she said, "You know that's not what I meant." Apparently, she should have said, "Marry a male lawyer or doctor." I think details really matter.)

I got a job interview in a beautiful town in Vermont, and we flew to the interview and I was sure I got the job. I was sure wrong. I didn't get the job, but in our overconfidence we had put the house up for sale and were getting ready to go when I found out about my wrongness. I quickly searched again, and after a phone interview with a school in Vermont, I was hired to teach computer technology to seventh- and eighth-graders in a middle school. I was concerned that although we'd visited another town in Vermont where we felt very comfortable with our raging crazy lifestyle blaring though our blazers, other towns might not be as accepting. I mentioned my concerns to the principal, who immediately put my mind at ease. It was a welcoming, open community that would surround us with love. We rented a house near the school and moved from Ohio to this town in time for the start of the 2001-02 school year.

As we pulled into town in our moving truck I noticed that many of our soon-to-be neighbors took pride in Vermont. State pride! So much pride that their motto was, "Take back Vermont." Odd, isn't it? Then, much less frequently, we saw a few signs that said, take Vermont forward. Make up your mind, state of Vermont! We were perplexed. After a little Googling we found out that the civil union situation that we had thought was embraced by the state, was actually quite hairy. The people against the homosexual takeover of Vermont were the Take Back Vermonters, and the people for the adaptation of the complete homosexual agenda, of which I never received a copy, were the Take Vermont Forwarders. Eventually I collected both bumper stickers and just culled it down to my bumper sticker, which simply said, Take Vermont.

Before the school year began, Sharon and I arranged for a justice of the peace to come over to our rented house and perform a civil union. This was of course so that Sam was safe and Sharon's if something happened to me, which was actually looking more and more likely the more we drove around our new neighborhood and tallied up the Take Backs against the Take Forwards.

The very comfortably dressed lesbian justice of the peace came and civilly unionized us in a very speedy ceremony in our back yard. She seemed a bit itchy to get going. The ceremony consisted of myself, Sharon, our son, Sam and a nervous lady. Pretty much how every girl dreams of her wedding day.

I began working at the school and fairly soon picked up a sense of discord and disdain. I gleaned both from the "Go away, lez," note on the whiteboard in my classroom. I reported this incident to the administration, and they flew into action. By "flew into action," I mean the assistant principal said, "Whatareyagonnado? Kids!" I was totally satisfied with this response. It was concise, to the point, completely uninterested, and all he had to say.

So back to teaching seventh-graders how to use computer programs. I had some really sweet students there and some others who I'm fairly certain are now residing in prison somewhere.

In class one day I noticed two boys snickering and whispering, and I asked them what was up. "Miss Baker, how come you don't mind your house being egged all the time?" I honestly had no idea what he was talking about. Later when I drove home, I drove around to see the front of the house. We didn't use that entrance and hardly ever saw it. When I say it was covered in eggs, I mean covered. There were shells everywhere and not a square inch that didn't have some egg on it.

At school the next day, the same boy and some of his friends brought it up again, asking why we didn't mind that the house was egged every night. It was sad, but I had to explain what "renting a house," meant.

"It doesn't really bother me because it's not my house," I said, hoping that this would of course make the egging stop.

"But you live there, right?" the leader asked.

"We are living there, but, it's not our house," I reiterated.

"But you live there, right?" he repeated.

"We rent it," I said.

"So it's yours," he said.

"No," I said.

"Why not?" he asked.

"We rent it, we don't own it," I said.

"So what's the difference, it's your house, right?" he said again.

"No, it's the owners' house. We pay them to live there. It's called renting."

"Well, it's going to be hard to clean up," he said proudly.

"I will not be cleaning it up, friend," I said, and then I watched him as the cog in his head turned.

"Well, be careful driving home today. It's a steep hill you drive down. Your brakes might not work too good," he said.

Funny kids! I was walking down the hallway later and ran into the seventh-grade counselor. "Hey there, just for fun, wondering how seriously you would worry about a seventh-grader who implied he was going to do something to my car?" Obviously this was a silly concern because he was in seventh grade, for heaven's sake. "Well, depends on the seventh-grader honestly," she said. I told her the kid's name and she said, "Hmmm, you might want to be careful. His father is in prison for cutting someone's brake line." Well, holy shit. I did drive carefully that day, even went down the street that cut in front of the house instead of farther down the steep hill, just in case. It was the first time in a long time I had seen the front of the house. There he was, standing in the daylight, hurling eggs at the house. He waved as I drove around the corner. It wasn't a scary wave, just a kind of "Hey neighbor" wave. I waved back.

There was another student I had I truly wanted to adopt and talked to Sharon about it, but since he was not up for adoption, I was not legally allowed to take him. He was a sweet, lovely boy who you could tell just wanted to grow up really fast and be on his own. He would say the funniest things to me that I didn't understand until I looked them up on the Internet. This was not a boy who handed in his homework without prodding, but each day he would say something in response to the request for his work that made me smile. Some of my favorites were

"Miss Baykah, why you harshing me?"

I had no idea I was harshing him, let alone why!

"Miss Baykah, raise up off me."

Again, no idea I was anywhere near him.

"Miss Baykah, why you rassing me?"

At first I thought he was saying I was erasing him, but I later decided he meant harassing him. Technically, if you are a teacher, it's not harassment to ask for homework, technically.

This kid just made me smile all the time. He seemed to know that what he was saying was funny, and he used a tone and smile that made me feel that we were actually quite cool with each other. He was also the only kid who left me notes telling me who was egging that night or who was leaving rotten notes on the wall.

There were some more serious offenses that happened in that town that made it more than just a pain in the ass. Various events proved more frightening. Although I taught in the middle school the high school was attached and those students would walk by my class many times a day. Several times I took note of a boy who stared at me and had a grimace on his face. Eventually this got very annoying and I went to the hallway and confronted him. "Is there a reason you are standing there staring at me and not going to your class?" I asked him. "Yeah, I don't agree with your lifestyle," he told me. "I don't remember asking. Go to class." I told him. He then went on a rant about Jesus or God, it was someone all-powerful that was shockingly only focused on my family and me. By the time he was finished a large crowd had gathered. I heard other high school friends of his asking him what was up. "She's a dyke," he told them. One of his friends said, "She has a kid too." The big mystery and the comment that made us get out of Dodge, (not the town's real name) was made by a boy who never had the nads to admit he said it. His response to hearing I had a child, who was two at the time was to say, "Not for long." I must admit you must have tremendous self-confidence to know you can take on a two year old. I stared at the boy that started it all and thought to tell him that his bigger concern should have been that his mom was his aunt but I realized that was not his fault. Also, soon when he looked in the mirror he would notice he was balding, and that friend, is not normal for a high school kid. So we set about getting out ASAP.

I suppose we should have cared more about that house, and we did feel bad that the house was egged, but we were also just a bit peeved about how the house had been described by the owners. They clearly had just wanted to rent it out and sold us on the fact that it was "totally childproof, not a worry you should have." This house actually would have been more accurately advertised as the Museum of Ass-Ugly Fragile Owl Knickknack Housed in All Glass Cabinetry House subtitled Death Trap for Toddlers. We could not relax in that house until we created a mini room inside the family room with an octagonal playpen system that kept the curios out of Sam's reach. The owners had an arrangement with a neighbor who would come over every time it snowed a lot and get the snow off the roof. One day Sharon and I were hanging out with Sam watching TV, and we heard the fella climb up the ladder and get on the roof. Then we heard a loud noise and a tumbling as the man rolled off the roof. Sharon looked outside and asked the guy if he was okay as he hobbled across the street back to his house. He left the ladder, and later when the snow thawed a shovel fell off the roof into the backyard. How we got out of that town alive is a miracle.

CHAPTER 28

Goodbye Joey

There are people in your life whose impact and presence is so immense that their absence seems incomprehensible and incredibly unlikely to ever happen. But then they do go and you are left to figure out who will or can fill that enormous void. Sometimes the answer is that no one can. Sometimes you realize that no one will. Sometimes you realize no one should even try.

One month ago today my father, Joseph G. Baker left this world. Since then I have felt the need to write about him but kept getting overwhelmed. Overwhelmed with grief, overwhelmed with memories and emotions. Where would I start, and would I ever stop writing? I realized today that I won't write just once about him, how could I?

So I write today, for the first time, about my father who is no longer here. *

Joe Baker was my first introduction to the concept of Protagonist. If my family was a story, Dad was the protagonist, the hero, and the supporter. My father was my friend, he was my advocate and he was my role model for almost every area of my life. All of my life, when I have not sure how to treat someone in my life, I've thought about what Joey would have done. When a situation troubles me, I've thought of how Joey would have handled it.

I know it's common to canonize the loved ones we lose. I am not doing that. I remember the entire man.

I had arguments with my Dad about many things. Politics: not our thing. Once as a birthday present I showed my Dad how much I loved him by photoshopping (before that term existed), my image dancing with Ronald Reagan. That's a lot of love. The arguments we had were few, but intense. We always came back to an understanding that we would agree to disagree with a person we loved deeply. In this life I have had many things happen that I regret. I am lucky though in that I was fortunate enough to spend almost all of my father's last weeks on earth near him. We talked, really talked, and although I had told him so many times how much I loved him, I needed that time with him to say it all again. I thanked him for being such a great father. I thanked him for giving me confidence. I thanked him for loving me. And I told him again how much I loved him. I also told him that I did not want him to go, but that I knew he had to. I let him see me cry, I let him see what his being gone would mean to me. I told him to go and that I would be ok, that we all would be ok. The last time I saw my father alive I was sobbing and I held my hand against his stubbly face and although he had not woken up much that day he opened his eyes and spoke very clearly. "Why are you crying hon?" I told him that I had to go back to Vermont and his face lit up and he said, "Ok, I'll come too!" I said, "Ok, let's go," and I kissed him and held him and he went back to sleep. I have had several people in my life die but none have died while I was there. I wonder if they all knew something I didn't. Like maybe I just couldn't handle it. I don't know. I talked to a social worker that worked with the hospice people and I told her that I worried that he would die after I left and she advised me to tell my dad when I was leaving and let him make the choice. I don't know if I believe that he chose to die when I was not there, maybe he did. When my mother died, I felt upset that I was not there at her side, but with my dad, I am so grateful that I had the time with him that I did. Nothing left unsaid. It's rare to be able to say that. I am lucky to have had that and even luckier to have had the father I had.

I'll love you forever and think of you every day my dear Joey.

so much love

your daughter

Jane

* Written in 2011

CHAPTER 29

A Pearl of Wisdom From My Daddy-O.

(Me=Second from left, in the sporty one piece)

My sons were arguing recently and it was a brand new never before argument. Sam and his friends didn't want Max and his friends bugging the big boys. This was a perfect time to reveal some sound advice provided to me by my father.

"When I was young I wanted desperately to be included in my brothers games in and around our yard. One day when I was around 8 years old my brothers provided me with such joy by allowing me to take part in a game they were playing with some of the other neighborhood kids. I don't know the exact name of this game but I do recall that some of the kids were Bears and some were Lions. I was to have a pivotal part in the game and was to roll in a ball and play a lion turd. "Lion turd!" they screamed as some of them attempted not to step in/on the turd…me. After a few moments my father came out and stood next to his little turd daughter. "Jane, you look like an ass," he said.

"But Dad I want to play!" I pleaded with him.

And here is where the wisdom comes in.

"Jane honey, get up! Whenever you want to do something so bad that you are willing to pretend to be a lion turd to get it, you need to think to yourself, 'Would Dad say I look like a chicken's ass?' and if the answer is 'Yes' you need to not do it."

So I got up and started my game of war and I was a general in command of the war-ness!

I played alone. But alone I was the General, not a lion turd!

I told this story to my sons when my younger son was acting similarly pathetic trying to play with the older boys.

It had the desired effect. Both boys have called me "lion turd" all day.

My father was so much better at life lessons!

CHAPTER 30

It Happened One Day

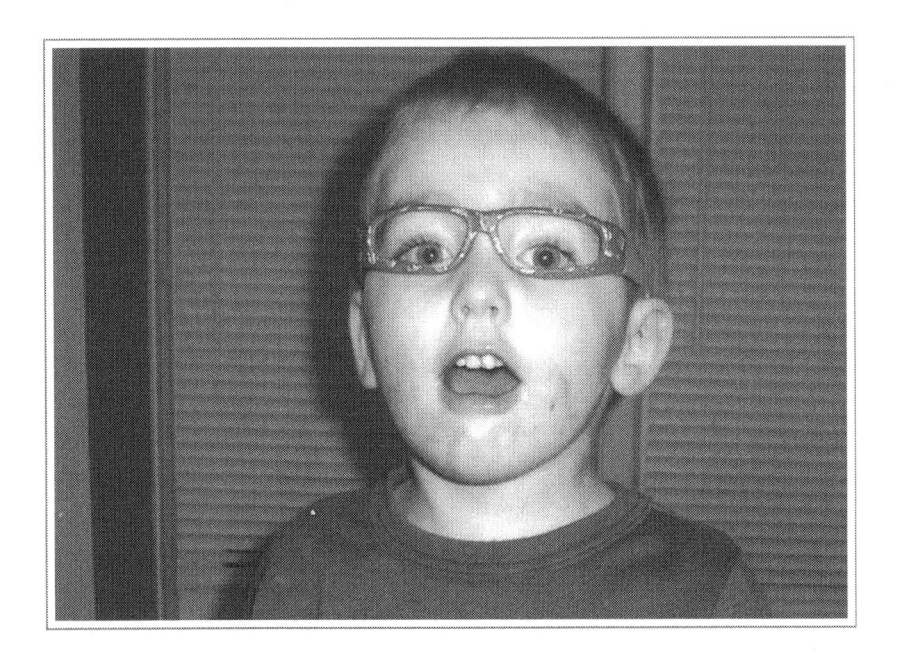

Sleepovers are fun, usually. In 2006, when my son, Sam, was five, he had a sleepover with his friend Patrick on a Saturday night. When I came into the living room in the morning Sam asked me to help him change his shirt because it hurt to lift his arms. When I helped him I saw that there was a significant lump halfway between his shoulder and his neck, near his collarbone. It struck me as odd, and I called Sharon to come look at it. She did so and we thought we should call the doctor. Our regular doctor was on call at the emergency room, so we drove to Brattleboro Memorial Hospital from Putney to meet her. She said that the lump was "impressive." She had some blood tests done, and Sam was given antibiotics by IV. The doctor came in with the test results and said, "Well, it's not lymphoma and it's not leukemia."

I heard Sharon mumble, "Oh, that's great." I was shocked that these things were on both of their radars. He had a SWOLLEN GLAND, for God's sake! He finished up the IV, and we went home with a prescription for more antibiotics and a diagnosis of cat scratch fever. Yup, I know, Ted Nugent, but it turns out it is a real illness. And guess what? You get it from the scratch of a cat, and it causes a fever. This is an illness that I can respect: it's very clear!

A few days later the lump, although smaller, had not gone away completely, so we saw the doctor again. More antibiotics and yet after a few more days, the lump was still not gone. The third visit to the doctor ended with Sharon and I being clear that we would be relieved to have an X ray done just to know nothing else was going on. The doctor was fine with that and told us to head down to the hospital and she would let them know we were on the way. We drove the forty-five minutes to the hospital and waited patiently until it was Sam's turn. The technicians were very kind and allowed me to go into the room because Sam was scared. It only took a couple of minutes, and we landed back in the X ray waiting room. The technician told me it would probably be around twenty-five to thirty minutes for the doctor to read the X ray. We played cards and read while we waited.

After forty minutes had gone by the receptionist said that there was a call for us. Sharon took the call and returned to tell us that it was our doctor and the hospital radiologists had said that they had seen "something" on the X ray and that now they wanted to do a CT scan. My stomach twisted and I felt light-headed and panicked, Sharon looked terrified, yet we both smiled and told Sam that we had to do one more test. Sam wailed when they put in an IV for contrast. I just wailed inside. These technicians were also kind enough to let me stay with Sam during the test. As he screamed and cried I sang him a song I had been singing to him since he was born. It was a lullaby written by Cris Williamson. I had always loved this song, and it always calmed Sam down.

When we finished this test we returned to the waiting room and were told that this test might take forty-five minutes to an hour to read. Around two hours later we saw our doctor walk into the waiting room. She looked terrible, and as she got closer to us I knew I had to get Sam out of there quickly. I grabbed him and ran out the back of the waiting room and bolted for the parking lot. A cab was out front and I threw Sam into it and climbed in behind him.

"Go!" I said.

"Wait, are you Eileen Shafer, did you call for this cab?" the driver asked.

"Yes, that's me, now GO!" I yelled.

"Okay." He pulled away quickly as I looked out the back window to see Sharon and the doctor running after us.

The cabdriver looked suspiciously at me, "So, we still goin' to Belmont Ave?"

"Um, no, instead take us to the bus station, no, the train station, please." I said.

He dropped us at the train station and we went in to see what trains were due in. A train to Boston was in a half hour, so I got tickets on that. When the train arrived Sam and I boarded and I let Sam pick where we would sit. He grabbed a window seat and began to count the trees we passed by. As the train moved faster he had to give up counting.

"You did great counting there, Sammy." I said.

"I got to thirty-seven or forty, I forget," he said.

"That's pretty high up there," I said.

I stared at Sam watching the world zip by and was so happy to have gotten him safely away. Sam made watching someone look out the window interesting to watch. So full of wonderment and joy at every single little thing he saw.

My amazement over my son's beauty was interrupted by the conductor asking for our tickets. I gave them to him, he punched them, and when he handed the stubs back there was a note.

I opened it and read it.

"We know why you are here. We want to help when your boy is asleep, bring him to car 28."

I looked around to ask the guy what this was about, but he had gone. Sam was not tired, but I knew if I sang to him and scratched his back, he would probably take a nap for me.

"Come here, Sam man." I said.

He climbed up into my lap and I scratched and sang, and soon he was sleeping. Sam does not sleep lightly; you could drag him through the snow and he wouldn't wake. I picked him up and headed toward the food car, just one car ahead, to ask about car 28. When I got there I asked which way I needed to go to get to car 28. The woman behind the counter whispered so as to not wake Sam. "Sorry, there is no car 28, 28 didn't latch on this trip, some problems with electrical I think, but ... if you are looking for someone who booked a seat that said car 28, they were probably seated in 27 or 29, both of which are back the way you came, four or five cars back."

I thanked her and she made a cute little pantomime to indicate that my sleeping boy was cute. I thanked her for that too.

Sure enough, I passed through car 27 to find car 29 right behind it. No car 28. "Not funny," I thought to myself. "I'm having a really bad day, and someone is playing pranks." I thought I should at least walk through car 29. When I was in between cars, my boy woke up and said, "Hello."

"Hello, honey," I said back to him. "Not you, Mommy, her."

I followed his gaze upward and saw a beautiful woman looking down. The woman motioned for me to be quiet and threw a rope ladder down to me. Sam had fallen back to sleep, and I held him tightly as I climbed. As I got closer to her, I realized I knew this woman.

"Mom?"

"Yes, it's me, Jane. Keep climbing," my mother said.

When I reached the top, she took Sam from me and went into a room that I assumed was on top of car 27. My mother had died in 2002, so seeing her here on this train was beginning to freak me out. Inside this room everything looked brighter, electric, and more alive (if that's even possible) than any space I had ever been in before.

"He's becoming so handsome, Jane," my mom said while staring at my boy.

"He is, isn't he, Mom," I replied.

"So we don't have much time; I need to tell you something and you need to decide what to do, do you understand?" my mother said quickly.

"Mom, you died. How are you here? Where are we?" I asked, realizing I was lost.

My mother went on. "We don't have time, Jane. Here is what you need to know. The doctor who was coming toward you when you ran, she was going to give you terrible ... if you choose, we can change that."

"Yes, Mom, please, do that, do that!" I begged.

"Let me finish, Jane. You will have to let us transfer his illness to you," my mother said sadly.

"Okay, Mom, that's fine. Do that, please. What do I need to do? I'll do anything," I said.

My mother explained, "You just need to ask me."

I was confused. "Ask you what, Mom?"

"You have to ask me what is wrong," she said.

"Okay. What is wrong?" I asked.

My mother disappeared, and the train did too. I was holding Sam, he was awake, the doctor was standing in front of me in the Brattleboro Memorial Hospital X ray waiting room.

"Sam has cancer," the doctor answered.

CHAPTER 31

Daddy Day at Dartmouth

We went to DHMC on 4/6/06 for the biopsy and Sam was very brave. He cried a little bit when we were in the prep room. It was scary and strange, lots of machines and lots of new people. They were all wonderful and sweet to all of us.

When it was time to go into the operating room they let me carry him in. First I had to put an outfit on that Sam said made me look like a "spaceman" and "silly."

I carried him in, held him and sang while they put him to sleep.

I sang a song I have sung to him at bedtime since he was a baby.

It's by Cris Williamson called "Lullabye."

Like a ship in the harbor

Like a mother and child

Like a light in the darkness

I'll hold you a while

We'll rock on the water

I'll cradle you deep

And hold you while angels

Sing you to sleep.

By the time I had finished singing the Doctor told me he was asleep. I helped them put him on the operating table and a nurse escorted me out of the room.

Leaving Sam on that table was the hardest thing I had ever done in my life. It is an awfully helpless feeling to leave your child in the hands of others. I felt like I wanted to sell them on what a wonderful child this was to inspire them to try really hard to make him well. I wanted to tell them that if this boy stopped living that I would die too. I wanted to say thank you and so much more, but instead I was so overwhelmed by fear and sadness and no longer had to "act" funny and upbeat that I just fell to the ground sobbing. It is such an antithetical thing we do when we hand our children off to someone with a knife, drugs, and plans to cut them. What kind of mother leaves their child in this situation? A desperate one, and I was more desperate at that moment then I ever thought I would be.

The nurse was nice and helped me up and took me to where Sharon was waiting. I had to register at the desk in the surgical waiting room so they could reach us if anything were to come up and when the surgery was over.

The very nice elderly woman at the help desk looked up and said, "Can I help you?"

"My son is in surgery, his name is Samuel Baker-Gentry," I answered.

"And you are?" she asked.

"His mother," I replied.

We had been telling Sam that the treatment for cancer would involve some drugs that may make him lose his hair, but that it would grow back. In an effort to have him not feel alone in his coming chrome dome I cut my hair very short, shorter even than in the above picture.

"You mean, you are his father?" the much more elderly than I had previously understood.

"Um, no I'm his mother." I insisted. "Please may I have a beeper?"

"I will give you a beeper but you are not his mother!" she stated again.

"Ma'am, I swear that little boy came out of me, I was there, I saw it!"

She looked closer at me and said, "Well you can't be his mother because his mother is over there!" She pointed to the other side of the waiting room where Sharon was already sitting.

"I am Sam's mommy." Then I pointed to Sharon and I said "And that's his momma. Please may I have the beeper?"

"Yes, of course, but I'll have to give you the father beeper, I already gave the mother beeper to her."

"Fine, I'll be the dad, I don't care." I knew the woman meant no harm and at that point she could have called me pond scum as long as she called me when we could see Sam.

With both mommy and daddy beepers in hand, we waited for a couple of hours until the surgeon and Sam's doctor came to talk to us. The surgery went as expected, it would take several days until we would get the official report. About an hour went by and they let us be with Sam, he said he was tired and wanted to go home. So did we.

CHAPTER 32

You're a Mother

On Mother's Day I am reminded of all the things my mother said that I swore I would not repeat. Some of these things I have not repeated, others I have been shocked to hear myself say.

Here is a sample of the former, and I am proud to say I have not repeated these.

"Are you going OUT in that?"

(Caveat, I have two young sons, they have not yet tried to offend me with clothing or piercing choices.)

"Real world, real world." This was not an enticement to watch MTV; this was a statement that implied that I "was dreaming."

I rather like to think my kids are dreaming and dreaming fun and wonderful things. My mother was more reality based. It's one way to go I guess.

This is a small sample of the comments I have not made to my kids, but I am proud that they have not slipped out of my mouth.

Now for the sad news, the following things I have repeated, probably more than once. Like a car crash you cannot turn away from, I could not stop the phrase once it left the station.

"Why do you want to live like pigs?"

I realize now that my mother was not assuming that we desired to live like swine but rather that we did not care enough to clean up. My children do not care if the world thinks they smell, or are slovenly, or messy, if their hair looks like a terrible experiment. In my children's defense, they are still too young to care. My mother was still saying this to me when I was in college.

"Stop fighting." I was so sure my children would never fight because I would tell them that they are lucky to have each other and they would defend and love each other enormously. Wrong. Now I find myself saying even more things I swore I wouldn't because my initial plan backfired.

These things include:

"I don't care who started it I'm ending it."

"I don't know how to split a malt ball exactly in half, and I don't care."

"No, calling your brother a 'particle' is not inherently offensive but when he knows you are saying something to annoy him it will do the job!"

And for my many friends who have taken the journey to hell that is Childhood Cancer here are some things I never even knew I should hope not to have to say to or hear from my children or spouse.

"Emla will make the needle not hurt honey." Me

"Emla makes me feel weird Mom." Sam

"When do I get cancer?" Max, when he turned 6

"Is it bad?" Sam anytime anything hurts.

"Honey you can vomit on me, it doesn't matter." Sharon to Sam

"Wow, why did I wear crocs today?" Sharon to me.

"Ha, I knew you were joking on me." Sam after first surgery, checking his hair and being fairly certain we were kidding about his hair falling out. We were not.

There are so many more statements particular to the childhood cancer experience that I will stop there.

And lastly, I give you; things I never ever thought would come out of my mouth in my life and didn't even know enough to hope to avoid them. All of these were to, or about, my boys.

"Because you don't need an atom bomb!"

"You should never order $80.00 worth of nano pods."

"Wow, that is a serious amount of Old Spice Max!"

"He will seriously be the death of me."

"I can't love anyone or anything more than I love you."

"Yes, I love you even though you have a french fry hanging out of your nose."

"I think 'hands out of the pants' is a good rule for almost ALL of the time."

"I don't think it's fair that if your brother just said his character has invisibility that you claim your character has the ability to see the invisible, I'm sorry, I don't."

"It's fine if you hate me and think I'm a terrible parent, but you may not jump out of the second floor to see which bones are bouncy!"

"Seriously, hands out of the pants! You will never be president if you can't stop that!"

And a couple last things to say:

To my mother, I hope you are at peace and well and holding hands with dad.

To my kids, you make me appreciate my mother.

You also make me realize how lucky I am.

You both make me understand, more than anything else, the possible answer to the always-present question "Why am I here?"

I used to call my mother on mother's day and say, "Thanks for having me!"

To my kids I say, "Thanks for coming to me."

Made in the USA
San Bernardino, CA
17 May 2016